Letters from Flanders, written by 2nd Lieut. A. D. Gillespie, Argyll and Sutherland Highlanders, to his home people; – Primary Source Edition

Alexander Douglas Gillespie

LETTERS FROM FLANDERS

A.D.G.

Oxford 1911

LETTERS

FROM FLANDERS

WRITTEN BY 2ND LIEUT. A. D. GILLESPIE
ARGYLL AND SUTHERLAND HIGHLANDERS

TO HIS HOME PEOPLE

WITH AN APPRECIATION
OF TWO BROTHERS
BY THE RIGHT REV.
THE BISHOP OF SOUTHWARK

WITH PORTRAITS

LONDON
SMITH, ELDER & CO.
15 WATERLOO PLACE
1916

SECOND EDITION

'*MY good wishes and prayers go with all my friends, who have been so loyal and loving to me.*'

To these, his '*loyal and loving*' friends who are still in life, and to the memory of those who, like himself, have laid down their lives, this book of his letters is dedicated

TWO BROTHERS

AMONG many delights which store the memory of a schoolmaster the delightful picture of two brothers sharing to the full the golden age of boyhood at home and school has a freshness and radiance all its own. The two brothers are differently equipped: one runs up the school and wins the prizes; the other makes little of his books and is described as 'not so clever as his brother, but a very good sort.' Yet in my remembrance of some three or four pairs of brothers at Winchester it is always a peculiar joy to recall their intense loyalty to one another; each admired and loved the other for something he could not do or possessed not himself: the cleverness and distinction of the one; the steady common sense and judgment of the other: the brilliant career of the one; the sole motive of duty for duty's sake in the other. There was an invariable something which made you feel they were, each of them, really the same in different expression, one in ' the red ripe of the human heart,' each the complement of the other. And we discover that the secret and spring of this deep unconscious loyalty is love of home and home associations; we have here the simplest instance of true corporate life.

Alexander Douglas and Thomas Cunningham Gillespie were the only sons of Mr. and Mrs. T. P. Gillespie, Longcroft, Linlithgow, grandsons of the late Alexander Gillespie, of Biggar Park, Lanarkshire, and the late Thomas Chalmers, of Longcroft. They were both educated at the preparatory school, Cargilfield, Cramond Bridge, and afterwards at the two St. Mary Winton Colleges (Winchester, and New College, Oxford).

We all remember Douglas and Tom Gillespie at school. Douglas came to Winchester in Short Half 1903 : he had been placed seventh on the Roll for College in the July election. He moved up the school rapidly, and was half-way up Senior Division of Sixth Book, second of his year, in Short Half 1906. In 1908 he won the King's Gold Medal for Latin Verse, the King's Silver Medal for English Speech, the Warden and Fellows' Prizes for Greek Prose and Latin Essay. He was placed second on the Roll for New College in December 1907, and went up to Oxford in the following October. There he proved himself to be intellectually one

of the most distinguished men of his generation,
winning the blue ribbon of Classical Scholarship, the
Ireland, in 1910.

If he wished, he might have stayed in Oxford
and taken up the work of fellow and tutor of a
College ; but he was very definite in his desire
to come out into ' professional life ' and to read
for the Bar ; he wished particularly to devote
himself to the study of International Law.

He loved every hour of Winchester and Oxford ;
and then the crown of it all was the nine months' trip
he took with his father after leaving Oxford.   They
visited East Africa, China, Corea, Canada, and the
United States. I can never forget Douglas' letters to
me *en voyage*, nor the talk we had about it all when
he came back. Those who knew him and all who
read the letters in this volume appreciate his freshness of mind, his sense of humour, his grip of a situation, his love of nature, the knowledge of men and
things and their history which his wide reading and
intellectual alertness were fast developing. This
rare opportunity brought into play all these gifts
and powers at their best. Few fathers have had
such a time with such a son at such a moment of
his life ! It was a joy to think of them together
then : it is a comfort now to know that the father
has the precious memory of those days to treasure.

But Douglas keeps reminding me that I am

leaving out Tom, *animae dimidium suae* Tom
came as a Commoner to Winchester in Short Half
1906 · he began in Third Division of Middle Part
and sturdily worked his way up with the purpose
of joining Army Class and going to Sandhurst.
Douglas, I remember, came to talk over Tom's
future with me some time in 1907, and we resolved
that Tom ought to go to Oxford and enter the
Army as a University candidate. And so it came
to pass.

Tom was a beautifully made lad ; as he grew
up he seemed to be the type of Browning's

Our manhood's prime vigour ! No spirit feels waste,
Not a muscle is stopped in its playing, not a sinew
    un-braced !
Oh, the wild joys of living ! the leaping from rock up
    to rock,
The strong rending of boughs from the fir tree, the cool
    silver shock
Of the plunge in a pool's living water . . .

and the rest of it.

He rowed three years in his College boat, for two
of them he helped to keep New College head of the
river, and represented the United Kingdom in the
New College Olympic Crew at Stockholm in 1912.
He was always a keen member of the O.T.C. at
Winchester and at Oxford, and succeeded in
obtaining a University commission : he was
gazetted to the 2nd Battalion of the K.O.S.B.,

which he joined immediately after the outbreak of
the war. After three weeks' training at home, he
joined his regiment in France, shared the pursuit
from the Marne, was in the trenches at Missy-sur-
Aisne for seventeen days on the northern bank of
the Aisne, exposed to the fire of the heavy guns
night and day. Then he took part in the movement
towards the Belgian frontier and was killed in
action on October 18, 1914, near La Bassée.

Tom was a great strong, fearless, affectionate
fellow : his men must have believed in him and
loved him for what he obviously was to the eye
But there was much more in him than that. At
one time I saw something regularly of Tom's work.
At 5.15 P.M. on Wednesdays—an hour in the week's
programme I love to remember—he used to come
with others to learn something of the expansion
of our Colonial system, or British Dominion in
India, or the history of English commerce, or how
to read a book. I saw quickly that Tom had much
of that same insight and grasp of realities and genial
humour which made Douglas so sound and true.
Anyone who reads Tom's last letter, which is given
on p. 6, will see what depth of true feeling and
strong simplicity served to make him the son,
the brother, the friend he was.

Tom and Douglas alike were both stamped with
the same simplicity and strength of character

which won the confidence as well as the friendship of all whom they touched. They always made friends; more than that, they could do anything they liked with their friends, and they never liked anything but the things that were true and lovely and of good report.

Douglas had been reading for the Bar for some months and had joined the Inns of Court Cavalry before the war broke out The moment war was declared, as anyone can read in the opening letters, there was only one possibility for him, to give himself unreservedly to the service of the country he loved dearer than life. He at once enlisted in the 4th Seaforth Highlanders and was in training at Bedford for two months: he was given a commission in the 4th A. and S. Highlanders, and was attached to the 2nd Battalion on going to the front in February 1915. On September 25 he led the charge of his Highlanders in face of a terrific fire near La Bassée He reached the German trenches, the only officer to get through, and was there seen to fall.

' Glory to God, to God,' he saith,
' Knowledge by suffering entereth
And life is perfected by death '

I could not trust myself to speak of all that I expected of Douglas' future. Besides, Douglas himself would resent my petty speculations in the face of that supreme reality to which all his fine gifts and capacities led him and fitted him. The Great Cause claimed him as her own : and to her he gave himself in exultation.

It was just that buoyancy, freshness, entire absence of self-consciousness that made me so confident of his success in days to come. The highest usefulness of rare intellectual powers and fine promise are not seldom marred by staleness or overpressure or growing affectations or priggishness or the mere love of intellectual gymnastics. Douglas was as fresh and simple and direct to the end as he was the first day he came to Winchester, a wondering, fresh-faced, blue-eyed son of the land of his fathers. And he would, I believe, have kept that freshness of spirit through all his days.

Now he is gone from us, what message do these letters and the life that shines out from them tell ? The old simplest truths of human life, that duty is always possible, that self-sacrifice is sweet, that the love of home and friends and nature and fellowman is the crown of life. But he also reveals throughout the secret which makes self-sacrifice not only the law but the joy of true living. He can exult and feel composed and happier than he had ever been, because it was just everything without reserve—home and comfort and safety and brilliant prospects and life itself—he offered to the

Cause that claimed him ; losing himself in the larger purpose, he found himself it was ' deep calling unto deep ' the deep of his country's uttermost need called to the deep of his loyalty and devotion.

When that which is perfect is come and we see things as they are, we shall know fully what we now surmise, that the real tragedy of human life is to potter through it, carefully ' economising ' the little grains of faith, the feeble sense of duty, ' to loiter out our days without blame and without use ' ;

> Nothing of scandal or crime you see
> We have not murdered or robbed for pelf
> Just given poor work where the best might be,
> And over all is the trail of self—
> The curse of futility.

There was one heartache ; he knew that he himself was happy enough and his own life fulfilled, but he felt it was a hard trial for the dear ones waiting and watching at home.

For them the trial is not so hard as it would have been without the irresistible appeal of his courage to them to be courageous, to give as he gave without faltering, with a song on his lips : not so hard, since they catch the glow of his unclouded, happy life. Let Stevenson speak to them :

Yet, O stricken heart, remember, O remember
  How of human days he lived the better part
April came to bloom, but never dim December
  Breathed its killing chills upon the head or heart.

Doomed to know not Winter, only Spring, a being
  Trod the flowery April blithely for a while,
Took his fill of music, joy of thought and seeing,
  Came and stayed and went, nor ever ceased to smile

Came and stayed and went, and now when all is
    finished
  You alone have crossed the melancholy stream,
Yours the pang, but his, O his the undiminished,
  Undecaying gladness, undeparted dream

At times when we are oppressed by the sordid
or the seamy side of life and are tempted to despair
of human nature, let us turn to these letters and
thank God we knew and loved and worked for lads
like these : whenever we think of them, we think
of the love and joy of life and Peace that passeth
understanding.

HUBERT M. SOUTHWARK.

BISHOP'S HOUSE,
  KENNINGTON PARK, LONDON, S E
    March 20, 1916

PORTRAITS

LETTERS TO HIS HOME PEOPLE

I hope to reach Rhiconich on Tuesday 11th, though really prospects look so black to-night that I should not be surprised if we were kept under arms, and not dismissed from Camp, where we go on the 2nd. It is pitiful to think that the blood of the Archduke should need the blood of so many others to wipe it out—though I suppose his murder was just the match to the powder magazine.

I don't see any means except a war to decide whether the Austrian or the Serb shall have the ruling voice in the Balkans, and I don't see where the war will stop once it has begun. Instead of being a frame to hold Europe together, it seems that this system of alliances is just a net to entangle us all. Europe will be crippled for thirty years if a great war does come—it might be worth paying such a price to have it driven into the head of every man in Europe that our present armaments

B

are insane—but that, I'm afraid, is just what a war don't do, because of the passions it will leave behind.

Inns of Court O.T.C., Persham Down Camp ·
Sunday, August 2, 1914.

I have just sent in my name through the Colonel for a Commission in the Special Reserve of Officers in case of mobilisation. . . . There was no time to consult you and Mother first, but I felt sure that, if the want comes, you would wish me to do anything that lay in my power to help, for I am free, and my career at the Bar would not suffer from waiting for six months or so. . . .

We have no news to-night, and so I hope that there may still be some honourable way to peace. I don't want to fight the Germans, for I respect them, but if the country is drawn in, I feel I must go in too, and do the very best I can.

In the meantime we shall stay here, training and manœuvring for all we are worth. Good-night.

London : Monday, August 3, 1914.

We were turned out at 11 30 last night, after a couple of hours in bed, and hurried back to London by troop train—packed up in dark, leaving tents, horses, &c., and got here at 6 A.M. Till 4 this afternoon we were kept at H.Q. waiting for orders, but are now dismissed till to-morrow morning.

(*Later*.) After the news to-night and Sir E. Grey's speech in the House, I'm afraid there is little doubt that we shall be at war to-morrow.

All day long I have been thinking of you and Daddy, and wondering what you were doing and saying, for I feel that your part in these troubles is so much the hardest of all. We have so much excitement to keep us busy, and so many cheerful companions that it isn't hard for us to see the bright side of everything. . . . To-night we shall sleep well in our beds after our travels last evening.

How one thinks of all the Navy men who are working for us to-night—there must be a Providence to guide us out of all these troubles.

Good-night, with all my love. . . .

Royal Hotel, Weymouth : August 30, 1914.

You will wonder what I am doing here, but I made up my mind that, if I got the chance this week-end, I would run down and see Tom ; a lucky thing too, for when I got up to the Citadel this morning, I found that he was under orders to leave for France this evening, and I have just seen him off to Southampton, in charge of a draft of ninety-three Borderers. It was very short work, and I don't

B 2

think he had time to write to you, for he only heard himself this morning ; but you can imagine how well they think of him if they send him off so early in sole charge of so many men. Portland is a queer place. I never knew that the land rose to such a height at the end of the Bill ; it was almost like Hong-Kong, and the top has been in cloud all day. I slept in Weymouth, and walked over this morning. Tom was of course desperately busy, running in and out of other people's rooms to get some kit together, for his own has never turned up, except his sword. All the other fellows were green with jealousy, but gave him what he wanted, and I think he was completely rigged out for active service before he left. I lunched in the Mess. Then at five o'clock, every one turned up on parade. A wet fog had blown up from the sea, but it didn't damp anybody's spirits. Tom looked splendidly fit, with his revolver, field-glasses, &c. strapped about him, and his little bonnet cocked on one side, and he was very cheery in spite of a stiff arm, the result of his inoculation. The men fell in, in full marching order, a sturdy lot of fellows, who looked as if they meant business. Tom went round with the adjutant, inspecting rifles, kit, and boots, then he called them to attention with a roar, fours by the right, quick march, and off they went ; a pipe and drum band in front played

for all they were worth, and the men swung out
of barracks, and down the hill, followed by
tremendous cheers. It was a good long column,
and they were not small men, but I could see Tom's
head and shoulders standing up above their bonnets
as I walked behind. The officers were all at the
station to see him off, but I went on to Weymouth,
and had another chat with him, as he came through.
They were joined there by drafts from the Royal
Scots, Wiltshires, and Dorsets, and must have been
about four hundred in all, a big crowd to see them
off, and the Brigadier shook hands with Tom, and
wished him luck. I hope he will come back as a
captain, and I'm sure he looked fit enough to march
to Berlin. He has a lot of postcards in his haver-
sack, so no doubt you will hear from him soon.
He is likely to be at the base for a day or two before
he moves up, but of course he didn't know where
his battalion might be. I enclose his address for
letters, parcels, &c. If Mother will send a good
thick pair of socks, I'll make up a little parcel with
some plug tobacco and chocolate, and send it off at
the end of the week. I don't suppose it's any use
sending large parcels, not at least until we know
more of his movements.

(T. C. Gillespie overtook his battalion, 2nd
K.O.S.B., on September 10, took part in the Battle

of the Aisne, and was killed near La Bassee on October 18. The following letter, his last home, was received two days after the news of his death)

October 16, 1914

MY DEAR DADDY,—I wrote a hurried letter to Mother yesterday, but having some leisure time to-day, am taking an opportunity of giving you some more news. We have been moved from the Aisne right round to the North, and are now operating in the region we were originally intended for.

We had a soft time during our transit, and were kindly treated, so we knew we were in for something stiff. Nor have we been mistaken. We marched up country for several days, and did 30 miles of the way in French motor transport wagons, which showed us there was some hurry. They packed us very close; it was fearfully dusty, and the springs were very bad. I have had more comfortable and clean drives.

We spent one night in a house in which some N. French refugees, quite good class men, were also stationed. They have to get out when the Germans come anywhere near, as they are one of the reserve classes, and may be wanted. If they stayed, and the Germans got into their towns, they would all

"One feels one is doing something at last"

From letter of September 24, 1914

be made prisoners. We all had dinner together in style and were very friendly.

We moved on the next day and were billeted that evening at a castle, where we were entertained most hospitably by a French lady and her daughters, and I actually got a night between the sheets. It was a paradise there. Heaven and Hell are close together sometimes ; we were in the latter not many hours after leaving the castle.

Next day we attacked the Germans in the afternoon and advanced a considerable way. They gave us a pretty hot time though, any amount of bullets flying, and one company lost two officers killed dead and one wounded. At dusk I found myself with two platoons rather ahead of the rest of the line (I had started in reserve, but things got mixed) near a cottage and a trench of French soldiers. There were German snipers loosing at us close ahead We entrenched there by night. I had the Frenchmen under my command too, as all their officers had been killed. I found two poor fellows lying fearfully hurt in a ditch with several dead, and managed to get a bottle of wine out of their packs for them without the sniper getting me.

Fortunately a captain came and took command. Next day, having been about all night digging, I was shifted to make room for some other company.

I advanced to a cemetery to defend it and stayed there most of the day. It is a beastly thing to have to do, digging trenches among graves and pulling down crosses and ornamental wreaths to make room. One feels that something is wrong when a man lies down behind a child's grave to shoot at a bearded German, who has probably got a family anxiously awaiting his return at home.

We were at the edge of a village and the Germans were entrenched about 200 yards on. One could see heads in the trench sometimes, and sniped at them. There was a large brown barn door behind one man, a look-out, I think. I and a corporal had several shots at him, and later in the day I noticed through my glasses a white cross scratched on the door. It is a grim thought, but you have to think of individual Germans as a type of German militarism even if they are not.

The church tower also was fired at by us, the belfry windows being our object. If everyone agreed only to treat churches as such, one would feel more comfortable.

We slaughtered a lot of Germans in the failing light, who advanced in close order along the road. Then we had to quit, as the post was too advanced for the night, and the Germans came in.

It was a miserable day, wet, and spent in a cemetery under those conditions. There was a large crucifix at one end. The sight of the bullets chipping Christ's image about, and the knowledge of what He had done for us and the Germans, and what we were doing to His consecrated ground and each other, made one feel sick of the whole war (or sicker than before).

The next day we spent lying in the trenches there, with little to do except lie low, as shells from the Germans and, I fear, our own guns too were dropping near us. Towards evening a party of about forty Germans charged the left of our line from about 300 yards away. They made a noise like 'All, All' when they came out of the wood, 'Deutschland uber alles,' I suppose.

Mad fools they were to charge like that across a wet beetroot field. They must have thought about ten of us were there. Barely ten of them struggled back wounded. All that night we spent expecting to be attacked. Nothing came though, our bayonets were not inviting. In the early morning we were relieved by French troops. I have never talked French so fast or volubly as to get them in before dawn broke. They would stop and talk. The last I saw of that place was the shattered crucifix standing up against the dawn, and the glare of a score of burning homesteads all round.

We were marched back, a muddy, wet, tired, and hungry crowd, to rest. We lost two officers killed, one died of wounds, and three wounded, besides a large quantity of men. But our reward was to come when we got into billets—a letter from Sir Charles Fergusson, Com. 5th Division, saying that the Corps Commander wished him to express his great appreciation of our conduct and grit and courage, saying how proud he was of us and thanking us. Sir Charles added that he was all the prouder as we were all Scotsmen, and he said he would come and see us when we had had the rest and sleep we needed. He told our C.O. that he couldn't praise us enough. So 'something attempted, something done,' earned us a night's repose in billets. We were only supposed to be in Corps Reserve and were shoved in in an emergency.

Mails and mails came in, as we had been without for days. It was a case of 'save us from our friends,' as we had nowhere to put things except inside or on us. Still, thank you very much indeed for everything. *I* got all my things on. I got about 4 lb. of chocolate, which was delicious after bread about three weeks old, bread green with mould which I had one day, and jolly glad to get it.

We are in reserve to the 14th Brigade to-day, and very glad to rest.

I wish I had a table to write at, I could write better and at greater length.

Hope you are all well. I don't know when you will see us home.

Tom.

(A. D. G. had been in training at Lincoln's Inn with the Inns of Court Cavalry all through August, but after his brother left for France, becoming impatient of delay in getting a commission in a cavalry regiment, he enlisted as a private in the 4th Seaforth Highlanders, and was at Bedford with them till the middle of October. He then accepted a commission in the 4th Argyll and Sutherland Highlanders, with whom he was stationed near Plymouth and at Sunderland till he went to the front in February.)

In the train—4 30 P M   February 19, 1915

This morning a wire came from the War Office that Duff, Tyson, and myself were to proceed at once to join the Expeditionary Force. We shall spend the night in London, and go down to Southampton to-morrow morning. I only heard the news at 10 o'clock, and I thought I would not wire to you, for you would not have had time to see me here ; and neither you nor I would have liked to say good-bye on Newcastle or Darlington platform, or even to-night in London. For no one likes saying good-bye, and you and Daddy know how much I think, and shall always think, of you without my saying it. As I told you when I was home, it somehow does not seem to matter much whether you are actually in the room with me or not, for I feel that we are never very far away from one another these days. Of course I know what this news means to you at home—for we have all the fun and excitement—and you have all the waiting, which is far, far harder, and it makes me ashamed that I have been so impatient with my own little worries at Sunderland, when I think how brave and good and patient you and Daddy have been all these months. I was always proud to be your son, but you have made me prouder than ever—and you and Daddy must remember when I am in France that my greatest help will always be to think of you at home, for whatever comes I shall be ready for it.

Of course you know that ever since I saw Tom go off, and before that, I have been longing to go too, and do what I can. Once when the Colonel asked me, before Christmas, I told him that I did not want to go at once, but later, after I had been home, I told him I was ready, for other subalterns are married, and no one can hold back ; however, I am glad to think this wire came straight from the War Office, for it is best to wait for orders in your turn.

And now you will know all the time how glad I am to be young, and fit for something, whatever news you get of me ; when a man is fighting for his country in a war like this, the news is always good if his spirit does not fail, and that I hope will never happen to your son.

Of course I will write as often as I can, and will let you know at once my regiment when they tell me at the Base.

We have just passed Durham ; we shall not meet there this Sunday, but I shall always remember our week-end there, and I have liked to think of you and Daddy and Daisy together for this afternoon, and happy.

You mustn't think this letter a gloomy one, for I am as happy as can be, but there are times when I must say all that I am thinking, and this is one of them.

Good-bye then, with all my love to you.

Saturday, February 21, 1915

I don't think the Censor will tear up my letter if I tell you that I am on my way to Havre.

I left London early yesterday, that I might look in at Winchester on my way to Southampton, and Hutchie[1] and I had a very cheerful dinner with the Headmaster ; but when I got up to the station there, the train was an hour and a half late, and even when it did start, it settled down

[1] 2nd Lieut R. H. Hutchison of the 8th Black Watch, Scholar of Winchester and New College, Oxford, and Fellow of Brasenose. he was killed in action in France on October 13, 1915.

again at Eastleigh. I was in despair, with visions of courts-martial if I was not on board at the proper time, so I jumped into a train for Southampton West. There was no cab there, so I ran a mile at full speed, only to find when I arrived at the docks at 12 30 that the Havre boat was not likely to start till 7 A.M.—nor did it.

However, I'm on board now with all my belongings.

Southampton Water was full of torpedo-boats, transports, and hospital ships, and now we are out-side steaming south, but changing course sharply every quarter of an hour, as a protection against submarines. It's a beautiful day, blue sea and sun, with a lazy swell rolling in from the Atlantic. . . . We are a scratch collection of all nationalities on board—Belgian soldiers, French captains, and subalterns of almost every regiment. This is not a transport, but the ordinary cross-Channel boat.

Winchester looked just the same as ever. I walked down Meads at 5.30, and it was still quite light. . . .

Rouen Base Camp, 27th Division Details:
February 22, 1915.

We arrived here about 10 this morning—a bit of heath, two miles out of Rouen, with pine-woods all round—something like Surrey, except that there is the slight, almost indescribable, change in colours and smells which warns you that it is France. We took almost the whole night in the train from Havre, and slept peacefully in a siding for a couple of hours this morning. The station was a curious sight—full of trucks labelled ' biscuits,' ' jam,' ' rum,' and so on, while the varieties of uniform were even more extraordinary—Zouaves and Belgians, Indian orderlies, Tommies in sheepskins, officers in khaki turbans from Indian regiments, red-breeched Frenchmen, all waiting patiently for orders. The camp is enormous I don't know how many divisions have their bases here . . . They don't seem to have any orders for us yet, so we may be here some days. It is again a beautiful sunny spring day—they say there has been almost constant rain, and the mud is very deep in places, but here we are dry enough. In the distance is Rouen, and the spire of the cathedral, with the wooded hills on the far bank of the Seine ; and all round about are rows and rows of huts and tents. We are the farthest out of any except the convalescent camp, which has a pitch among the pines—the patients in their blue suits and red ties are all enjoying the sunshine.

We have a mess, but it takes a long time to get anything to eat, for there are so many coming and going.

Rouen : February 23, 1915.

To-day the 27th Divisional Base is moving across into new quarters—huts about a mile away—but I hope that Tyson and I will be able to go straight to the 4th Divisional Camp, which is older and probably more comfortable. We had a great bit of luck yesterday afternoon in getting hold of revolvers. The Ordnance Store was hidden away in the docks at Rouen, and on our way we met several other officers coming back, having been on the same quest without success. However, we reached the place at last, a sort of ramshackle goods shed in the middle of a cabbage patch, and by good luck they had been rummaging round, and had just discovered a couple which had been lost. So now we are fully equipped.

This hunt for the Ordnance Store took so long that we had not time for more than a glimpse at the cathedral in the failing light, but it's a wonderful mass of stone, and I must go back there. Vespers were in progress, but the nave was very empty, except for a few figures in black. Of course French-women wear black a great deal, but still one sees mourning everywhere, and when you look at the length of line the French hold, and compare it with our little section, you cannot wonder at it.

Rouen is full of quaint old streets. . . . While

" We are just at the beginning of the struggle I'm afraid, and every hour we should remind ourselves that it is our great privilege to save the traditions of all the centuries behind us.

It's a grand opportunity, and we must spare no effort to use it, for if we fail we shall curse ourselves in bitterness every year that we live, and our children will despise our memory".

From letter of October 1, 1914

A. D. Gillespie

I was standing looking up at the cathedral, an old Frenchman came up and pointed to Tom's skian dhu, which I am still wearing. ' C'est un poignard, mon lieutenant ? ' ' Mais oui, Monsieur,' and I drew it for him. He was delighted, and saluted me with great ceremony when we parted.

I find it very difficult to tell a French officer from a sergeant, but the best plan is to salute everyone. . . . With us I think saluting is a matter of discipline, but with them of manners.

We could not help laughing, when we were dining at a hotel, to see an old French officer, a brigadier at least I should think by the gold braid on his cuffs, march in with great ceremony, taking salutes right and left, and then hastily draw a large bottle from the folds of his baggy scarlet trousers before he sat down. They are evidently more useful, these scarlet trousers, than appears at first.

There was very little of the hardships of the campaign about our dinner last night—*table d'hôte*, and excellent Norman cider—though I think some subalterns already fill their letters with adventures and I believe the men's letters are very funny— they have all to be censored, and yet they often sit in their comfortable tents, and describe how the bullets are whizzing round them as they write.

Discipline is very strict indeed, but otherwise

c

there is far more comfort than there was at Sunderland, when first we came there.

It's not quite such a pleasant day, a shower of hail this morning, and now it's inclined to drizzle; but I shall have a walk in the forest presently, and there it should be sheltered enough. This life does interest me; I could just stand all day watching the different faces come and go.

(*Later*.) I have been up to the orderly room, and am posted to 93rd (2nd Battalion) Argyll and Sutherland Highlanders.

4th Divisional Details, Base Camp, Rouen
February 24, 1915.

Captain Ramsay and myself are under orders to stand by, which means, I suppose, that we shall be moving up either to-day or to-morrow, probably with a draft from some other regiment. It takes about two days to get up to the front from here, and I think we shall have some hours in Boulogne.

Two days ago I thought the spring had really come, but yesterday morning there was a heavy fall of snow, and all the tents are white—they look very pretty with faint light showing through from inside, under a starry sky. We got extra blankets from the quartermaster, and slept very sound and warm, in spite of another fall of snow in the night.

This morning it is thawing, but sleet is still falling ;
a miserable day for the trenches. But after all
one can feel now that every day brings us nearer
better weather . . . I see plenty of rooks, and for
some reason wagtails seem to be fond of our camps.
I suppose they like the shallow puddles, and the
little scraps of food from the cook-houses.

Billets . February 26, 1915.

I shall be too tired and sleepy to finish a long
letter to-night, but I must begin it, for there is so
much that seems new in the first day.

We had a long cold night in the train, with much
jolting and stopping, and when I looked out, there
was the usual landscape of Northern France—
farm buildings and long rows of lanky poplars with
magpies' nests in them. Whenever we stopped in
the early morning, the men swarmed out of their
carriages and ran helter-skelter for the engine, or
some other engine, to get their tins filled with hot
water for making tea. I always thought half of them
would be left behind, for the train never gave any
notice when it moved off, but except for one or
two stragglers, I think all of them were pulled in
again by their friends.

When we got to the station where the train
was split up into sections for the different corps,

c 2

I was amused to see the Railway Transport officers.
(27/2/15) They were both New College men ; one a
very talkative Etonian, who was a History scholar,
and the other a College Wykehamist, formerly
Prefect of Hall ; they had both had various adventures, and I don't quite know how they had come
to be there, but there they were, managing transport
as if they had been at it all their lives.

Then we moved on again ; it was a bright, sunny,
windless, spring day, with a little snow still lying
in places. We passed a cavalry brigade on the
road beside the line, with their horse guns, the
men all very warmly wrapped up ; both they and
their horses looked splendidly fit. Apart from that
there was little enough sign of war, except the
empty bully beef cans lying in the ditch beside
the line, thrown there by innumerable troop trains
as they passed. Occasionally there were little bits
of trench and cars and transport on the muddy
roads, while when we came to stations there was
plenty of bustle, big guns on trucks, stores, hay,
mail-bags, A.S.C. transport wagons, and fatigue
parties. At last the train stopped at our place;
we tumbled out on to the ballast and sleepers beside
the carriages ; the double line ran on straight in
front, as level as could be till it came to the place,
I suppose, where it is torn up between the lines.
The country all round was mostly ploughed fields,

without hedges, dotted with red brick farms;
there were lines of straggly poplars too, and in
places the fields were smaller, quite like England,
with tall hedges, orchards, and cattle-ponds.

It was very warm in the sun, and quiet, except
for an occasional sound like someone thumping
a tub in the distance. We marched off led by a
guide, the Middlesex and Argylls together; there
was a narrow strip of *pavé* in the middle of the
road, then deep mud into which I saw one bicycle
plunge to the hub of its wheel, and on either side
a deep ditch, green with scum and duckweed. In
fact, all this low country can never dry up, for
there is water just below the surface, and ditches
divide the fields. The road was crowded—staff
officers in cars, Belgian and French soldiers, country
carts, peasants, for the land is all cut up into little
farms and there are red brick villages springing
up everywhere beside the old thatched houses;
but there were horses ploughing and men and
women digging in the fields as if nothing whatever
was happening. I saw an old Curé go past, holding
his skirts well up above the mud, till I could see
his fat black legs in stockings. We went through
two or three villages all full of men in khaki lounging
at the door of their billets. Sometimes there were
raw patches on the bricks round about the doors
and windows where stray bullets had struck in

street fighting, and there were one or two houses wrecked by shell. Some Tommies had patched up one of these, and painted on it in great blue letters, 'Breezy Cottage, this way to the married quarters.' Next door to it stood a shrine which had escaped untouched, with its own inscription, 'Notre Dame des sept douleurs priez pour nous'; these contrasts are strange.

We went on and on, between the ditches ploutering in the mud; the sound of tub thumping got louder; it was some of our heavy guns firing, but it was still calm and sunny, and several aeroplanes came buzzing over, shining in the sun. We crossed a bridge over a fair-sized river, and on again through new brick houses full of lean Highlanders, very like the suburbs of Sunderland, but somehow it was much more bright and cheerful. I could not help jumping when the guns went off, and some of the men were a little nervous too, but when one saw the old women knitting at their doors quite unmoved, one felt ashamed of it.

About 5 30, just as the sun was setting, we dropped the Middlesex and picked up a Canadian Pipe Band, who seemed to be wandering along with nothing particular to do, they played us into billets to the 'Campbells are coming,' which brought all the Belgians to their doors, and even our men picked up the step ; they were very tired with twelve miles of *pavé* and heavy roads, carrying full equipment, after their night in the train. Our billets are in a row of brick cottages, strung along a road, and I believe the trenches are about a mile and a half away. I am posted to B Company, where to my very great surprise and pleasure I found Captain Chrystal, who was with the 91st for three weeks, but has since been transferred. I also found Bankier, who was at Cargilfield and Winchester with me, though a good deal younger. The three others in our company mess are Hutchison, late of the K.O.S.B., and later from Rhodesia, where he had been farming ; he is in charge of the machine-guns ; Clark, second-in-command, who has just got the Military Cross ; and Boyd. The four of us sleep on the floor in a room together, and we mess there too, plenty to eat and drink, with cakes and sweets from parcels. Letters have just arrived, and I have Mother's p.c. written on Monday, and Daisy's letter to Sunderland from Longcroft, the first which have reached me since I left home ; very nice to have news of you.

We go to trenches to-night, and I must stop now to pack up ; it is raining and blowing, very different from yesterday, but I expect we shall settle in somehow for our five days and nights. The Middlesex come out when we get in.

I expect I shall be able to write a line in trenches, but if I can't, I will of course write again as soon as I come out.

March 1, 1915.

It was dark before we started for the trenches last night—the road was deep in mud, and crowded with troops—so that there were many halts, and much swearing at other regiments, who of course are always wrong. At last we got on to a clear space of road, and began to hear the rifle fire getting nearer. There were other signs too, wrecked cottages, and burnt farms. Finally we turned off the road, and squelched through ankle-deep mud and water. There were lights moving mysteriously ahead—they turned out to be braziers all along the line for the men to warm themselves, and cook their rations. We had a platoon of Canadians with us too, who had come down for one night to be instructed—but my platoon sergeant led me to the wrong place, so we had to turn along the line, wading knee-deep in mud. Just here we are not in trenches, but in breastworks—for the trenches have all been flooded out. I was posted on the left of the company, but the breastwork here is rather patchy, so that by daylight we are quite isolated, for the sniping is too accurate to make it worth crossing an open space without good reason. So we watch by night, and sleep by day, each man in his own post, or sleep for an hour or two anyway. . . . It was a cold night, with heavy showers, but bright moon between, so that there was little prospect of an attack. I spent most of the night on my legs, so that my feet did not get cold—but what mud! up to the knees in places, with pools of unknown depths—wretched for men, but they are wonderfully cheery in spite of it.

I had supper in the dug-out with the other company officers, and met a Canadian there, who was one of Jack Gillespie's subalterns in Winnipeg —curious, wasn't it? But at dawn we all began to keep down, and I had breakfast by myself, cooked by my servant—ham and eggs in the trenches!

To-day I have been sleeping or lying warm and sleepy, watching the clouds drifting very fast, and aeroplanes racing through them even faster— it's funny to see them plunge in and disappear, and then come out again after their dive. Of course I can only look towards our billets, except for a very occasional and very hurried glance over the top towards the Germans, who are about 400 yards away here. . . . I wish I could draw better, but I must practise. . . . I send you a little scrawl of a sketch, which will give you some idea of what I see—a couple of wrecked farms, a stretch of beetroot field, rows of tall poplars, and the distant spires of a much contested town   There was heavy fighting here in October, but very little since, and we are losing very few men, in spite of all these spells in the trenches. The guns have been banging away hard all day, but they fire over our heads and don't trouble us, they are so keen on ' busting ' one another.   Well, I am afraid you will find it hard enough to read this, but fingers are cold, and I am writing on the back of my diary, balanced on my knee . . .

Dug-out   March 1, 1915.

Daddy's parcel of gum-boots arrived last night ; they should be very useful, for after ploutering about in this mud, one can't lie down in boots and putties, and though waders are admirable for sleeping in, I could never move in them once I got into the depths. Last night I went over for supper all together to the dug-out, and we had quite a cheery evening—it is nice to see someone after lying alone all day and we have plenty of sweets—and a three-course dinner—also I had my first taste of army rum—for I have to stand by and see a lot of that served out to the men as soon as it gets dark.   It's fine strong stuff and warms

you up inside, but I think they should arrange
that men who don't want it could get chocolate
or some other small thing instead. I gave my
letter to Mother to a subaltern who came down
with a digging party, and I hope he remembered
it. For two hours we were busy filling and carrying
sand-bags—an awkward job in the dark, but you
can't show yourself by day. It came on to blow
very hard with rain too, so to-day I have treated
myself to breakfast in bed, and lunch in bed too—
there is really no point in getting up, for I can
only move ten yards—and here I am quite cosy,
when I have finished wrestling with my boots, and
changing socks. All these operations are difficult,
for there is barely room to sit upright—and the
puzzle is to bring one's legs inside with as little
mud as possible on them. It might interest you
to know what I wear—two thin vests, and shirt,
your old woolly, an oilskin waistcoat, my tunic,
and that very thick-sleeved waistcoat Mother sent,
on the top of all—then I have put on trews, one
can't lie down in a kilt without waking up to find
it round the neck . . . and my feet are rattling
about in the waders, which are large enough to
allow me to exercise all my toes, and keep them
warm. . . . For breakfast I have ham and egg
and tea ; for lunch some ' Maconochie '—that is
a kind of tinned stew—very good—and we are all

grateful to Robbie's namesake, whose name is on the tins—bread, cheese, marmalade, and some bun, which Clark gave me—so you see I'm beginning to take quite an interest in talking about my food—and eat enormously. . . . I have with me too Dante's ' Inferno,' but with eating and sleeping, and writing, I can't find so much time to read, and I have military books too, and your letter which I got just before coming down, I have read again and again. . . . I'm glad to think of you so busy at Hopetoun, and now that I have come out, I'm glad you can get some afternoons at home. . . . I see blue sky again, and the cold wind is dropping. . . . You can imagine how we count the hours till we shall find ourselves back in billets.

Much love to all; perhaps I shall get some letters to-night.

March 2, 1915.

This is a very quiet day so far, even the snipers seem to have got tired of wasting ammunition, and though the guns were banging away this morning, I slept through it all, for we had been very busy with a new breastwork in the early hours. This is said to be the quietest part of the line at present ; we are about twelve miles north of the place where Tom was killed. All last night we heard the guns muttering away to the north—a very heavy cannonade—and they were noisy in the south too.

It's not very warm yet for March—there was a furious storm of snow for about half an hour yesterday afternoon, and frost last night, but I am keeping fairly dry, which is a great thing. I'm afraid those boots are no use; they would do very well for slush or water, but this mud pulls them half off the foot at every step, and finally one of them tore when I was trying to fix my heel into it firmly. However, I am getting hold of a pair of long gum-boots from the sergeant-major. At one time the trenches near here were considered the best on the western front, and Sir John French and Poincaré both came down to see them; then a fortnight's wet weather ruined them entirely, and so the game goes on. I see very little of the men all day, they sleep and sleep, but at night they sometimes talk. There is one funny old Irishman, who is in charge of the grenades. He is very anxious to put one of his shirts on the Kaiser, and then tie him up to a stake—' Ye would see him wriggle then, with them biting, and him not able to come at them.' . . . You can guess what ' they ' are; fortunately there seems a good chance to keep clear of ' them,' if one is careful.

We shall get a bath, I think, when we get back into billets, and I hope to hear that Tyson has come up to join us. . . .

Trenches   March 3, 1915.

The guns on both sides have just been making things very lively for one another. The shells make a scraping sound, rather like stones sliding down a rocky gully. When they 'bust' in the distance, I see a bright flash, and then a puff of greenish-grey smoke, which drifts away slowly in the wind. It was very wet last night—but so far I have always managed to keep the upper part of me dry, so I have been warm and comfortable all day, sleeping to make up for time lost at night. There are working parties almost every night, so I am usually on my legs for several hours—just as well to get some exercise, and I think this constant lifting of the legs in deep mud, must develop new and strange muscles. I have been censoring the men's letters—it seems almost too bad to read them all, but some of them write so nicely, that one is glad to know what they are really like, under a rather unpromising surface. One wrote to his wife, thanking her for a shirt, but saying he wished she was here to 'scratch his back as she used to do'! Most of them just want 'so and so' to know they

were 'asking' for them. . . . I got two postcards
from you last night—one from Sunderland, and
one to the base camp—very glad to hear of you—
the parcel from Toronto has not come yet—no
doubt it will—and to-night I think some of your
other letters will reach me. . . . An aeroplane
has just been buzzing overhead—one of our own,
I think They are like hawks in this war, and where
they poise and hover, you know there will be trouble
for those they see underneath, for they signal to
the guns. Fortunately our own airmen seem to
have the measure of the Germans and chase them
always at sight. . . .

The Brigadier came round last night, shook
hands, asked all about me, and was very affable.
The 91st are in a bad place, it is they who have
been losing the officers whose names you see in the
papers, not we. . . . I have never managed to
write to Gwen at all since the base ; you must
copy some letters for her—if you can read my writing
at all. I cannot write well lying on my back,
and the only typewriter here is the machine-gun—
the men's nickname for it.

You must not worry yourselves about me, for
I should be very happy out here if it were not for
thinking of *your* being unhappy.

Billets : March 5, 1915.

I got your letter two nights ago in the trenches,
and this afternoon I have had one from Daisy,
and two from Mother, one of them forwarded from
the base camp at Rouen—so I am doing very well,
and am very lucky to have people at home who
can write me such good letters, for I look forward
to them very much. . . . We got safely out of
our trenches and breastworks, and marched back
to billets—about four miles along very muddy
roads, and slippery *pavé*. I was tired and slept
very sound—the excitement in the trenches keeps
you going, and when it is all over, you suddenly
feel that you have been living very fast. The
Germans have two or three search-lights, which
throw a dazzling light across our lines all of a
sudden—but I think their light shows as much to
us as it does to them. I think, too, that they are
more frightened of us than we are of them, for they
are always sending up flares and coloured lights,
as if they expected to find us making a night
attack.

We have flares too, but hardly ever use them—
and we never fire if we can help it, which makes
them uneasy, for of course they know that we are
always there. No one in my platoon was hit, which
rather surprised me, for they would stand up and

cheer when they saw our guns knocking the houses
to pieces behind the German lines—and that of
course is the sniper's opportunity. I quite agree
with you that an officer ought to save himself
when he possibly can. In the trenches here, every
life lost is sheer waste, for no one need get hit, and
it's not like an advance, when someone must get
the men on at all costs. So I take every care, and
am not afraid of being thought afraid—for that's
a piece of cowardice rather worse than the other
kind, and has cost us many lives in this war. . . .
I am keeping a small diary, which I bought hurriedly
in Sunderland—it must be made for the meanest
kind of business man, for I was amused to find it
left no space for Sundays, but had instead several
sheets in front for 'notes of articles lent.' . . . It's
wet and windy, so I am just spending the day in
billets—and to-morrow I shall go into the town,
and try to get a bath We are only a few miles
from the place where Ronald tried to escape. I
find that when I wear the kilt in the trenches, I
get quite like ' Rex,' for the mud splashes up about
my knees, and hardens in little lumps—and when
you try to pull them off, out comes the hair too.
. . . There is not much elegance about our billet;
this room has a bare floor, bare walls except for a
hideous frieze of grapes and vine-leaves painted
round the top, and a mirror, damp and blurred,

D

with a line where someone has drawn on it with his fingers ; then over the mantel-piece, or rather the stove, is a case of everlasting flowers, and two gilt china jugs, which can only have escaped breaking by a miracle. . . . But it's a nice cheerful place compared with the trenches—and now that Captain Chrystal has gone away down the line to recover from a chill, I spread myself on the floor, and the others sleep upstairs, in *beds*, if you please ! !

About parcels, things to eat are always welcome —jam, marmalade, potted meat, cake, fruit, just as if I were back at school again ; we all share everything together, so I have been living very well. It's difficult to buy anything in this wasted country. I think I have all the clothes I want at present, but I should like a book or two to read and throw away. I have been reading the ' Inferno,' now I think I'll make an effort to finish ' Paradise Lost '—there's a cheap Milton in my room, I think— send the first volume first—and Scott's ' Bride of Lammermoor,' which I don't think I ever read— or any other Scott in a cheap edition—in fact anything solid, for I don't think sixpenny novels would go down so well at present.

I shall write every day while we are stationary here, but of course I may not always get the letters posted, and they may arrive in bunches.

Billets · March 6, 1915.

Really I do not grudge the Middlesex these last two days in the trenches. It has rained in torrents, and blown a gale from the south-west. . . . I'm afraid it gives me nothing but pleasure to watch it on the window, and think that I shall sleep under a roof to-night. This morning the General was to have inspected us, but it was too wet for him, so we did nothing at all We have a gramophone, a very good one, which is kept busy. . . . Then I went into —— to have a bath—it's hard to remember not to write the names of places. First of all there are new raw suburbs of red brick —very like our own in manufacturing towns, except that the brick is less dingy, and there are lines of blue and white and coloured bricks for ornament above the doors and windows The rain had almost washed the *pavé* clean in places, so that the red stone showed through the mud. We crossed the railway line—along which we must all have passed that first year on our way to Switzerland. The rails are rusty, and grass is growing between the lines. Then came the town itself— rather like the city of a dream. The houses are mostly brick, painted white and blue, with wooden shutters—which makes them look as if made of cardboard, all the more so when you suddenly

D 2

see one without roof or windows. Most of the
glass is broken—shutters closed and windows
boarded up. Every here and there was some
great gap where a shell had burst through the wall,
and set the building on fire I noticed sand-bags
along the pavement, up against the gratings and
cellars—to which I suppose the wretched inhabitants fly for refuge whenever the German shells
begin to drop in the town. But most of them have
now fled altogether, and the streets are almost
deserted except for our own soldiers. The clock
in the town hall was stopped—a great hole in the
dial—but some shops were still open, and I saw
quite a smart milliner's window full of hats and
toques, and the ' Café du Sport ' was full of patrons.
We had our bath in a private house—a fine spacious
building with a hall full of palms and shrubs and
singing birds in cages. It was strange to tread
on carpets again, and see a polished floor, and there
were still some French servants in the house,
carrying linen up and down stairs. There were
a great many cloth and linen factories in the town,
and it must have been a prosperous place once,
but now, as I say, the empty streets and shuttered
windows made me feel as if I was walking through
it in a dream. I don't want to blow anyone's
house to pieces, but when I see these ruins and the
light of the burning farms at night, I wish with

all my heart that they were German houses, and German farms. . . . Mrs. Haldane has kindly sent me a present—a little pocket hairbrush and comb, and some phials of iodine. The Flemish mud is very dangerous in the slight wounds sometimes, the fields are all so heavily manured and the country so populous. . . . I do hope we shall succeed in taking Constantinople—the effect throughout the whole of the East would be enormous, and it would let all the wheat from the Black Sea get out to us—at present things look well. . . . Your letter was a great pleasure. I like to hear of all the little things you are doing every day.

A four-course dinner is just coming in, so I shall stop for to-night.

Billets . March 7, 1915.

Two letters have come from you since I last wrote, I think—and they were a great pleasure. I notice when I am censoring letters that men don't write to their fathers very often, but to mothers and sisters a great deal, and also to ' dear old pals.' It's rather a shame somehow to read all their letters, but they do write and write, even if it's only to say ' hoping this finds you well, as it leaves me.' It ' leaves me ' in billets, after another day's rain. I went to service in the morning, Established

Kirk, held in an old school ; the singing was very
vigorous, with two cornets for an accompaniment.
A padre out here should be of the very best. For
men need some help, when they are set down in a
strange country, with nothing to do all day in their
billets, once their kits and rifles are clean—and it
makes one very sad to see a man drunk out here.
Why can't we do as the Russians are doing, for the
war at any rate ? I like French wines myself,
but I'd be glad to give them up . . . Most of my
platoon seem to be decent fellows—of course I
don't know all the names yet, but I must get to
know them all, in and out, or set out with that
idea—and then, at any rate, I shall know something
of them. There are very few regular soldiers left
now, mostly reservists and special reservists. . . .

Hopetoun must be a very beautiful place, and
there can be no view in the world to beat that view
of the Forth. . . . I hope some time we shall all
have another holiday at Rhuveag. What a jolly
time that was last June ! and what an age back it
seems in the past now ! I remember saying to you
how nice it was to think that it was only June,
with four months of summer still in front of us
Still, we both have something better to do than
take holidays at present, and I only wish I was as
competent for my job, as you are for yours. . . .

As I write a curious patter comes in from the kitchen where the servants use the stove to cook our dinner—French and Scotch, and then very slow and deliberate French with a Scotch accent. . . . The Germans near here behaved very well when they were in billets, and paid for everything. One is glad to know it.

I find that Boyd, one of the subs., was a ' wet bob ' and rowed in the Eton VIII—so of course he knows all Tom's friends—and is a big jolly person, with a tremendous laugh. I believe Roger Hog's battery is not far from here. I wish I could run across him. Well, as you see, there's very little news from the Western front, but we all keep smiling, and are growing fat.

Billets . March 8, 1915.

I was glad to have your letter of March 5 to-day —how quickly the posts come through—we sometimes get the *Daily Mail* the day after it is printed. Yes, I think things are going pretty well, although you probably get more news than we do—the corps publishes a summary of information every day, but there is very little in it for obvious reasons. It is dry at last, though very cold, with occasional snow showers from the north, but if the wind holds, it should have made a difference in the trenches before we go in to-morrow night. The others have gone to ———, so I am staying in billets in case anything should happen—but even the guns have been very quiet these last two days. Somehow one quite forgets in billets that one is only a mile or two away from the German lines, and that they could shell the whole place to the ground if they felt inclined. Of course it's not worth their while to do it—and anyway there are so many houses, that even a spy would find it hard to direct them . . . I am feeling I want some exercise again, and must do some digging. I find that I sleep sounder on the floor than I ever do in bed as a rule. . . . I have just been for a potter in the garden at the back, to see if there is any sign of spring yet, but there is hardly a green blade, and this part of France seems to me just as bleak and bare as the east of Scotland—but the summer must be hot, for I see vines growing along the wall outside. . . . Everyone who was at Mons says the heat was terrible—roads very dusty, and *pavé* cruel to the feet—and the men had to throw away their packs before the end of the retreat. I hear nothing but praise of the way the Guards have fought throughout this war—they say they have never failed, and never surrendered. They have been cut to pieces again and again, so that none of the original Guardsmen can be left, but their name and their tradition has passed on to the new drafts, and their battalions are even more formidable now than they were at first.

A *Sphere* or an *Illustrated* would be interesting to me, and to the men afterwards ; that is, supposing we continue our present mode of life—but of course that can't last for ever, and some day there will be marching, as there was at first. . . . Here is a rough sketch of our room in billets I wish I could draw better, so as to give you the face of the old French woman in the kitchen—she seems to get on very well with our servants.

Trenches . March 10, 1915

I did not write yesterday, more laziness, I'm afraid, than anything else, for though it seems a busy day when one is packing up for the trenches, there should be little enough to do All our kit is taken away, and stored in case of a move, while other officers come into the billet, then when we come out, it is taken back again. . . . We started with snow falling fast, not a very cheerful omen ; however, it cleared off, and there was a keen frost, with a beautiful starry sky. The search-light was very busy, and the guns, too, through the night. To-day the frost is all away, and we have something

like a mild spring day   The birds have been singing
since our stand to arms, and various chaffinches and
wagtails have come to look at me in my dug-out ;
if only we move in time, what an embarrassing choice
of houses to let they will find in this line of breastworks.   There has been a good deal of firing, but
I can now get along, by day as well as night, to the
rest of the company, so that the day has gone fairly
quickly, and the second time in trenches everything seems much less strange.   I have my proper
sergeant back from furlough, too. . . . I have been
getting all your letters, I think—it's nice that they
come so quickly.   I am very well indeed—no colds
or other ailments—and I sleep splendidly.   Well,
if I'm not so sleepy to-morrow afternoon I'll try to
write a better letter.   Everything in this life gets
to seem so natural that after the first few days I
wonder what there can be to say.

Trenches : March 11, 1915

Well, we have had another two days in the
trenches, and two dry days at that, so everyone is
quite happy.   We heard yesterday that the 7th
Division and the Meerut Division had taken the
first line of German trenches to the south of us.
I don't know how wide a stretch they took, but it
sounds good news.   The war will last a long time

yet, I expect, but every little success brings the end nearer ; this morning our guns were very busy sending shells over our heads into the German lines, and the German guns started to reply. They put four or five near my platoon, and one actually on the top of the breastwork, so that it buried a man underneath, but he was pulled out none the worse except for a shaking. We could not help laughing to see him plastered with thick yellow mud from head to foot, and after a tot of rum to pull him together, he laughed too—an old soldier, quite old enough to be my father, I think . . . I had a very nice letter from Laura yesterday ; she seems to have had enough ' trouble "since the New Year to entertain a third-class carriage all the way from Edinburgh to Glasgow; but I hope the babies are recovering, and that it is now well over. . . . This has been a very mild day, and as I write, during the evening ' stand to arms,' the birds are all singing in spite of the sniping, which still goes on. I can imagine how busy they will be at Hopetoun and Longcroft. . . . I have got H. S. Merriman's ' Velvet Glove ' to read, but so far I seem to have been busy digging, eating, or sleeping— you don't often get more than three hours together, but putting one nap after another you have plenty of sleep. Certainly it's a most interesting life out here   I wouldn't have missed seeing something of it, and it is good to think that we shan't always be in trenches. How I do admire all the officers and men who have had four months of them, and yet remain so cheery ; they do deserve well from their country, and the new army will have to do well to stand beside them.

Trenches : March 12, 1915.

We are having a most peaceful day ; it is still, and quite mild, though the sun hasn't broken through yet ; and we are all feeling happy, because we have had three dry days in the trenches, running. There was some heavy firing on our left early this morning, and I believe they have been doing well up there. You can see the flash miles away when they are firing heavy guns at night, and, of course, long before you hear any sound ; in fact, you often see the flashes when you can hear no sound at all. . . . A German crept out last night within one hundred and fifty yards of our lines and tied two French flags to a willow tree ; just a bit of swagger, I suppose ; they have been getting it pretty hot from our machine-guns lately. I have some terrible old grumblers in my platoon, but my N.C.O.'s are good enough, and I like my platoon sergeant, who is very slow and quiet, more like a real Highlander, of whom there are hardly any in this battalion, mostly from Glasgow, Falkirk, and thereabouts. The nights are very dark so that it is difficult to get much digging done, except by the light of the German flares and search-lights, which help us quite as much as they help them. Meals seem to have a great effect on the gunners ; they always have a round or two after breakfast, then, as a rule, they settle down again until they have had their lunch, when they begin again, and towards the end of the day our batteries seem to get the mastery, and the Germans make no reply. Is it the effect of tea, I wonder ? No doubt that is a forbidden meal in Germany now, because it's so English. I am very, very dirty, with mud splashed all up my legs, from wearing the kilt day and night ; but it has not been nearly so cold this time.

Trenches : March 13, 1915.

Last night was a great night for me, for two delightful letters came, one from yourself and one from Daisy. We always gather in the dug-out, where Clark, the company commander, sleeps, and wait eagerly for the mail. It comes in about eight o'clock as a rule, as soon as it is dark enough to walk up and down the road behind in comparative safety. The newspapers come in too, only a day old, and we settle down to dinner, which is usually the same—soup, stew, thin tapioca, *vin ordinaire*, if one cares to drink it, and tea from a battered tin coffee-pot. Bankier is

a sort of Wm. Whiteley, whose parcels contain everything from cigars to carriage candles. Please don't
think this is a hint that I want either, for I will let
you know when my supply of Sunderland candles—
8½d. for three pounds, and pink wax into the bargain—
begins to run short . . . Then we sit and smoke
while the bullets go singing overhead—they only
sing really loud when they are ricochetting—until
it's time to turn the men out to dig, or fill sand-bags,
or carry down planks and hurdles, which the mud
swallows up voraciously, like a bottomless pit. . . .
I haven't really taken to smoking again, but perhaps
Daddy will send me a box of cigarettes. You know
what sanitation is like sometimes even in a fairly
good hotel on the continent, and from that you can
guess what it is like in a small French farm like our
billets. . . . Things have been very quiet again to-
day, though there has been heavy cannonading to
right and to left of us, up and down the line, for we
have advanced in several places lately, and no doubt
the Germans have been trying counter-attacks
They haven't shelled us again; perhaps they are
waiting for Sunday morning, which is a favourite
time—but to-morrow night, if all goes well, we shall
be back in that bare ugly room, which seems a
paradise after the trenches. However, in spite of all
last week's rain, four dry days have really done a lot
for us, except that just at first the liquid mud gets

more sticky and tenacious when it begins to dry. . . .
I have been censoring the men's letters again, and
it's often very amusing, but they write so many
that it takes up quite a lot of time—they send so
many kisses, often to three different girls by the
same post, and they are fond of quoting poetry,
copied from cigarette cards, or sometimes their own
composition—and there are the usual Scotch phrases,
'lang may your lum reek,' and so forth, though, as a
rule, it's only 'hoping this finds you well as it leaves
me.' As to my letters, certainly make copies of
them if anyone cares to read them, and they might
be interested to see some of them in B.C. . . . It's
very nearly five, so that the long day will soon be
finished, and we stand to arms from dusk till dark.

Trenches : March 14, 1915.

We are to spend another day in the trenches
instead of coming out to-night, rather a disappointment, but we have had such fine weather that we
mustn't grumble. The mud is really drying up now,
and everyone is pleased with the good news from
Neuve Chapelle. Our losses are found to be pretty
heavy ; you can't attack entrenched positions and
wire entanglements without losing men, but the
Germans will have lost far more. I shan't get
your parcel with the hose-tops till I get back to

billets, so I won't be able to write and thank your soldier till then. It's well that you have such a family to look after, and that most of them seem so nice. They may say what they like about the east coast of Scotland, but I believe it has an earlier spring than the north-east of France. We have a favourite blackbird who sits up in the tree above us, and answers when the men whistle to him, no matter how heavy the firing may be, and the crop of grass inside this dug-out is growing very long and white, but otherwise there are few signs of spring yet. Rather a funny piece of news came round from corps headquarters yesterday; they said that a patrol had recently discovered a dummy figure between the lines, dressed up in German uniform, which exploded when they touched him, wounding one of them, so we are warned to be canny with lay figures; it would be so ignominious to be knocked out that way. We have picked up a German rifle grenade, a curious kind of bomb on a long copper rod, which is fired out of a rifle, and carries about 300 yards; only this one had not exploded. I hope they won't experiment any more with these things on our trenches when I'm comfortably tucked up at night, but there have been various alarms at night lately, so we have spent most of the time on our legs. I have finished H. S. Merriman's 'Velvet Glove'; he doesn't perhaps go very deep, but he can tell a rattling good story, which many of those modern psychological novelists, with their elaborate analysis of character and of sensation, quite fail to do. We have to report to-morrow night on the habits of the enemy opposite us, so I think I must write a little sketch of the German character.

Trenches : March 15, 1915.

We have had another day in trenches, owing to a change in the disposition of the brigade, and I don't think we shall have much more than three days in billets from now on—but now that the weather is so much better we shall be right enough. There is very little sun yet—to-day was grey and windless, but there was quite a touch of spring in the air, and I knew by the flies that were going about that trout would be rising on a still day on the loch, when you could see every ring. Yes, you will have to go up to Rhuveag, and see about the garden. I see plovers flying overhead here sometimes, but I don't think I'm likely to hear a ' whaup ' this April. I was amused to watch two old magpies the other day; they wanted to cross over from this side to the German lines, but every time they started to leave the row of poplars just below my shelter, there would be a crack from some rifle, and back they would turn, and perch again to chatter about it, until

E

they had picked up courage to have another try, and then the same thing would happen all over again. They are so very suspicious that they are much more frightened by sounds than the smaller birds—we have a good many chaffinches and wagtails here, as well as blackbirds and thrushes. All last night, starting from four o'clock, there was tremendously heavy firing to the north, the sky was quite lit up with the flash of the guns, although the firing was some miles away, and they went on all morning too with hardly a break The Germans opposite us fire very few rounds from the batteries now ; I daresay they have moved many guns to cope with our advance at Neuve Chapelle and elsewhere. Yes, it was interesting to see these pictures of Yuan-shih-kai at the Temple of Heaven, and very significant, I thought, that the top-hat brigade, who used to give fizz dinners at the Hotel des Wagons Lits when we were in Pekin, have all disappeared. Instead, they have gone back two thousand years for their dresses, and there was nothing Western about them at all. No doubt Yuan will found another dynasty, which may be a little better than the Manchus, but otherwise things will go on much as before. I don't think the Chinese, though they are so clever and well educated in their own way, take enough interest to get a very good one. What they seem to think of most is their family, including their ancestors, and, incidentally, the Emperor and his family, who are heaven-born, and so deserve respect. But as for government, they treat it as a necessary evil until things get really unbearable ; then they have a revolution, and a new dynasty, and the whole thing begins over again. . . . We have all been eating far too much, and I must try and get some walking while I am in billets, for here there is so little chance to move about ; at first I was all for digging, and carrying, myself, but on these very dark nights I find that work tends to slacken off in other places if the officer gets too busy in any one place, so now, as a rule, I just potter round, and have a look at everything, and then there is more to show in the morning. . . . H. S. Merriman talks of the ' Siren sound of the bullet, a sound which some men, when they have once heard it, cannot live without '; but I don't think I shall want you to fire volleys under my window to put me to sleep when I get home. I had a letter from an Indian yesterday, whom I used to know in London—very keen about the war. . . . Do you think there will be Christian service in San Sophia again on Easter Day, after 460 years ? With the extra thirteen days of the Greek calendar, I believe it may be possible.

Billets : March 16, 1915.

Here we are back in billets at last. The Germans opposite must have been relieving one another too, I think, for we had a very quiet evening, and handed over the trenches without difficulty. There are several hundred yards of very open ground to cross on the way up, and the men are heavily loaded, so that they cannot move fast, but all went well, and we only had to crouch down once while the beam of a search-light swung round over us. We are a disreputable gang of ruffians when we march back, even after six dry days. The men all have their goatskin coats on, or what remains of them, but they have so many straps and things to carry that you only see tufts of hair sticking out here and there. Some of them have braziers, bags of coke, waterproof sheets, and all varieties of woolly caps, and the most amazing styles of lower garments that you could ever imagine, for to keep their legs warm, in spite of the kilt, they have set to work with sacking and canvas ; some of them, too, have bought baggy blue trousers from Frenchmen, or patched up old garments that they have found lying about. I myself had a stubbly red beard of six days' growth, and a top dressing of yellow clay up and down my legs. Yet in the early days of the war men had to go five weeks without ever changing their clothes or boots.

It seems a very long way coming back over the *pavé*,
though it is really only a mile or two. But at last
I saw all the men housed in their new billet, a big
Flemish farm, where they climb up hen-ladders to
the lofts where they sleep, and was free to open your
letters and parcels. Since Chrystal is still in hospital
and Boyd is hit, I have been promoted to a bed, so
that last night I actually slept on it ; soundly too,
though it has a great slope. I never had such a luxury
at Sunderland. It was a nice mild night, so that
through the open windows I could just hear the
pop-pop of the sniper down in the trenches in the
distance, and see the glimmer of the star-shells. It
was pleasant to wake this morning with farm-yard
noises for a change, in broad daylight, instead of
watching the dawn break from the ditch behind our
breastworks. The garden has begun to sprout a
little in these last six days, but it has also grown four
gun emplacements, and a forest of young trees to
hide them from the airmen. . . . I think I must forbid
you to send any more parcels just now, for I have
already lost one buckle from my kilt, and shall lose
the others if we contrive to do nothing but eat sweets
all day. The room is just filled with little boxes, for
all the others have ' cargoes ' too. We shall do well
for the next week, unless, like the man in the Bible
who had goods laid up for many years, we suddenly
get orders to go marching off, up and down the line,

and have to leave everything except the minimum
behind. For we have not really done any fighting
here, though we pretended to attack one morning,
just to help things down at Neuve Chapelle, and it
is the 91st who have been in a hot corner up the line,
and whose names you will see in the lists presently.

Thank you very much for all the socks and
woolly things. I ought to be comfortable both
inside and out. But please send me some insect
powder or liquid; so far I have only met the
skirmishers, but supports and reinforcements can't
be very far behind, and I think a whole new army
will begin to move when the weather gets warmer
in April. It's no trouble, but a pleasure to me to
write every day, so I shall go on doing it while our
quiet life continues.

Billets : March 17, 1915.

We are changing billets to-night, and to-morrow
we go back into the trenches, so this time we have
not had much of a rest ; also a new captain turned up
last night, and took my bed! but I slept just as well
on the floor ; he was A.D.C. in Mauritius till Novem-
ber ; from such queer places do we gather officers.
Clark is just promoted Captain, so I think he will
still command the company. This morning was
still and bright and sunny ; I had a bit of a walk, on

dry roads too, for the last week has made a great difference, and I saw a dandelion in flower ; but what a smell there will be when the ditches dry up ; every inch that the water sinks seems to unclose a new smell, more powerful than the last. There are some nice old farms and cottages scattered about, in contrast to the red brick in the suburbs of the town. What I should really like now would be a fortnight ' trekking,' marching ten or fifteen miles a day ; it would be a great change, and would harden every-one up ; then, at the end, we should be ready for a fight ; for if we must lose men, it would be far better to lose them all at once. Instead, we have half a dozen killed or wounded every time we go down to the trenches, and a dozen sent to hospital, and so the drain goes on.

I had another bath this morning, and a walk to the town. I wanted to get some French news-papers, but I could only find an old *Matin*, with nothing in it except translations from the London papers. Then this afternoon, I had another walk with Tyson, to a village about a couple of miles away, which has been shelled almost to the ground. It's a melancholy sight ; of the church nothing remains except the skeleton of the tower, and a roofless nave ; many of the houses have simply been blown to pieces ; all have windows broken, furniture wrecked and burnt, wallpapers and scraps of window curtains trailing in tatters from the window frames. I'm sending a p c to your rifle-man ; the hose-tops he knitted are splendid, but my writing paper is all packed up.

Billets . March 18, 1915

We changed our billets last night, and now two companies and their officers, 500 men in all, are quartered in this old farm. The farms here are fortresses in themselves ; they are built all round a square courtyard, the middle of which forms a manure heap, the size of which I never saw equalled, in any part of the world   There is a big arched gateway leading in, with heavy doors to bolt and bar at night, and round the edge of the manure-heap, under the shelter of the eaves, runs a raised path.   Three sides of the square are given over to horses, cows, calves, pigs, sheep, and goats ; and the fourth side is the house proper, where the old farmer, his whole family, and all his labourers seem to live too.   You can imagine the confusion, when 500 soldiers have to find their way in too. They lie down in the stalls beside the cows, climb up hen-ladders to roost in the lofts, and curl up in any corner where they can put a bundle of straw. I found four horses in the place allotted to my men, and had a tremendous argument with the farmer and the farmer's wife, who refused to put them in beside the cows. So at last I made my men take them there, and then managed to pacify the old man, his wife, and his daughters, for I told them it was war, and that anyway we weren't as bad as the Germans. It's the first job I have had to do since I came out, which could not have been done equally well by a good sergeant. . . . My French is very fluent, and very bad when I get angry, but just good enough to get things done; for I know all the words when I can speak slow enough to think of them, and can make them speak slowly too; but as for pronouncing rightly, or speaking grammar, I'm quite hopeless. Of course the French here hate having soldiers billeted on them, and no wonder, for it turns everything upside down, even when the men behave themselves, which they do not always do; the finest officers and training couldn't make saints of men straight from Falkirk High Street and the south side of Glasgow. The officers' mess is a fine old room, long, with a low ceiling, looking out on the moat or rather muddy ditch, which runs round the farm on three sides. It's curious to think what a lot these farms have seen—1635 was the date over the door; this corner of France to-day is so very different from one's ideas of France under the Grand Monarque ;—but I suppose they have had troops of one kind or

another billeted in them fifty times before, and will
again, unless the Germans suddenly shell them
to the ground, which they might do any day. The
gunners have an easy time of it just now, except
when they go into the trenches as observing officers ;
otherwise they live in these farms two miles from
the firing line, ride about all day, and hear the
news. Of course, when they were covering the
retreat, they got blown to bits, but now the infantry
are the targets. . . . I wish the papers would not
make such a hullabaloo over a small advance ; we
did well, but after all the line is very much where
it was and the Germans are not broken, or anything
like it. The same thing will have to be done again
and again.

We go off to trenches in an hour or two.

Trenches : March 19, 1915.

We are in a real trench this time, one of the few,
I suppose, which has survived the wet weather.
It's really very luxurious, for the bottom is all
paved with brick, or boarded over ; and though
naturally there is still a deal of mud in places,
we are quite happy. It's very quiet too compared
with our last place ; there is no machine-gun fire,
and very little sniping, so that unless they get busy
with ' Percy,' their trench-mortar, we ought to

have a peaceful time. 'Percy' makes a great deal of noise, I believe, but does very little damage. Our (trench) headquarters are quite palatial; there is a ruined village about a mile behind the lines, which has been used as a furniture shop, so we have a table, chairs, a stove, cupboard, lamp, shelves, &c., and can even stand upright. Bankier and I share one very small shelter for sleeping; there's just room for the two of us to wriggle in, and one can't lie straight out, but in this cold weather that doesn't matter very much. It was clear enough at 2 A.M. when I lay down this morning, but at 4.30, when I got up again, there was a thick coating of snow, and snow still falling, and there have been heavy snow showers all day, and a bitterly cold wind. However, we are warm enough in our blankets, with books, cigarettes, sweets, and two mouth-organs; and the men too sleep all day, wrapped up in their fur coats. They certainly get plenty to eat; there are always tins and tins of bully beef to spare, jam too, and I don't feel very sorry for anyone who says that bully beef is very dry, or that he prefers marmalade. There are two rather nice old farms standing in orchards just behind us, but of course they are utterly wrecked, and the new grass is beginning to sprout among the fallen bricks. The Germans are about 400 yards away here too, but since we are in trenches, they

have very much less to aim at than they had in
our last place. We have a cat too, which is taken
over by each relieving regiment. I suppose it came
from one of the farms behind ; certainly we might
all learn from it how to adapt ourselves to this
life, for it seems completely happy. . . .

Trenches : March 20–21, 1915.

This letter never got any farther than the first
three words yesterday—why, I don't remember,
but we have two Terrier officers, both Staffords,
down here in this company at present, following
us round to be instructed, so that space is rather
limited. Both yesterday and to-day we have had
most glorious sunshine, the first since the day that
I left the train. It's very cold and frosty at night,
but by day the West wind blows softly, and the
grass sprouts from our trenches and parapets, so
that I'm now sitting out of doors in the sunshine,
in a trench behind the firing trench. There is a
lark singing high up between the lines, but in spite
of that the sniper is busy, and sometimes when an
aeroplane comes over, you see four or five little
puffs of white cloud in the blue all around it, where
the shrapnel from the air-craft guns is bursting.
Really we are very comfortable in this trench,
for it's a palace compared with our last one, and

the snow that we had two days ago melted almost at once. There has been comparative peace up and down the British front lately, and, so far as I know, no heavy fighting. But Boyd had very bad luck last night, for after a week in the field hospital, he had just left there to come back to us, when a stray bullet caught him in the leg, at least a mile behind the firing line. So this time he will go home, and not come out of hospital so quickly. Somehow, one doesn't feel very sorry for a man who gets hit, not dangerously, with a dressing station handy, and a doctor to attend to him at once ; for even if he feels the pain for a week or two, that's nothing much in the long run. I wish I could see Hopetoun park on one of these sunny days—last year I had such a short spring holiday, and then the weather at Rhuveag was as bad as it could be, until the day I had to go away. Yes, I remember the ' Melting Pot ' very well, and I suppose if the war ended next week, we might be doing just the same next winter, for the change, whatever it is, which will come after the war, will not come quickly, and least of all will one notice it in surface things ; though I don't think we know anyone who hasn't changed, and when I read of ' nuts ' who haven't enlisted, or people who still want to see the Derby, it doesn't mean very much to me, for they don't exist for me—I've never met them.

I don't think it's hard to explain why men get drunk; it's just as easy to drink too much as to eat too much, only you can see the effects of the one sooner; but it's hard to understand how they go on getting drunk and hopelessly drunk, when they know what it means. I like sharing a bottle of wine myself, but I wish we could do as Russia does, for this war. I have heard from Sholto, who seems to like Plymouth, also from Dick Mitchison, who must be a very smart subaltern now, and is chafing to get out. Something is wrong when a man with his brains isn't given a chance sooner; he shouldn't be a subaltern at all, but on the liaison staff, which links up the French and British armies. How he used to argue with Tom in the flat this time last year; and Tom used just to smile and fence away, and pretend to be a stupid athlete without an idea in his head. This letter might interest you; the writer is one of the best men I ever knew; people used to say he had a conscience like a roaring lion, but you want some people like that in the world, just as you want a sergeant with a sharp tongue. How beautiful the Dardanelles must be to-day if it is sunny there, and how attractive it must be to go round from place to place in the Ægean just now in one of our cruisers. You would see that my old friends, the 4th Seaforths, have been in some stiff fighting, but I'm glad that Tennant and Andy

Fraser are safe. We relieved one battalion of the Cameronians in these trenches ; their other battalion came out of Neuve Chapelle commanded by one second-lieutenant, the sole surviving officer out of twenty-three who went into the fight. If the great public knew these things, they might be better able to decide whether the British soldier, or the British thoroughbred, is in greater danger of extinction.

Trenches . March 21, 1915:

This is as fine a March Sunday as you ever saw, sunny and windless, so that you can almost see the new grass sprouting on the traverses and parapets. We have all been sitting basking in the sun, and the men have been stripping, and washing in what remains of the flooded trenches, so that they have got something out of all that water which made them so uncomfortable before. It has been very quiet too, except for the birds and the snipers ; there were several larks singing just between the lines this morning. We heard the song of the aeroplane too, at intervals, and the German guns have been very busy, bursting strings of shrapnel in little fleecy puffs : it must be great fun for the man with the anti-aircraft gun, and also very exciting for the airmen ; they say they hardly ever make a trip now

without getting a few bullets through their planes ;
but for all that many people say it's the safest branch
of the service. The cigarettes have come, and I
have been sitting lazy in the sun, and watching
the smoke of them. That's the worst of this life
in the trenches, you do get most abominably lazy,
so that you can hardly turn over in your blankets
without thinking about it for half an hour. It's
the want of exercise, I suppose ; but I had a walk
last night, up to the farm where the ration parties
go. It used to be a most appalling journey, three-
quarters of a mile in mud to the knees, but now it's
quite easy, and was a most beautiful starry night,
which reminded me of the nights at Nairobi. We
have two Territorial officers in our trenches to-day,
sent down to learn what to do ; perhaps they will
relieve us presently ; this division has never been
sent back for a real rest like the others, but has been
in and out of the trenches the whole winter   Will
you send me some nasturtium seeds ?   It would be
rather fun to plant them in the trenches here, now
that so many things are beginning to grow. . . . I
got hold of a German paper yesterday ; it had a short
account of a football match in Berlin, so did a
French paper of one in Paris the other day ; but
what interested me was to notice that they gave
very fairly and accurately the British Admiralty's
report of one day's operations in the Dardanelles,

except that they multiplied the number of our dead
by four—I know this because I happened to have
noticed the figures—and so had another subaltern.
That is just typical of their system in all their
reports ; they tell as much truth as they think
necessary to hide their lies—or, rather, tell as many
lies as they think their public can reasonably swallow.
My diary says that spring begins to-day, and when
I went along just now to look at the rifles and
ammunition of my platoon, I found two or three of
them wearing *chapeaux*—French girls' straw hats ;
they must have got them from some ruined shop
in the village behind us—the whole effect was very
funny, with the fur coat round their bodies, and gum-
boots on their feet. There are a great many flies
dancing about this evening, so I hope we are in for
a really good spell of weather. Great cheering down
our trenches just now ; the men always get hold of
the wildest war news in the evening, and shout it
towards the Germans, who reply with volleys if
they think it worth while.

Trenches . March 22, 1915.

We have another day of sun and calm, though the
frost again last night was very sharp, and the stars
extraordinarily bright. My feet have never been
wet at all these last four days, thanks to the bricks

from a ruined farm behind, with which our trench
is paved. There is a sound of melodeons and
mouth organs, mixed with the sniping, for many of
the men get parcels from home, as well as gifts from
different societies. They all have to be opened in
presence of an officer, for fear that bottles should be
wrapped up in socks and shirts. I think all your
parcels have been coming. I'm glad we did not have
so much snow as you, but how often March is the
snowiest month of the year! I hear there are over
seven hundred New College men serving ; and an old
Wykehamist, a Colonel of R.A.M.C., who was in the
school from 1844 to 1849, so that he must be very
nearly eighty. There have been a great many
aeroplanes overhead again to-day, and the usual
attempts to hit them with shrapnel ; it seems strange
that they succeed so seldom. I get very tired of the
perpetual rattle of earth from the parapet, when
the sniper hits the top row of sand-bags ; there's
no danger whatever if you keep your head down,
but unless they are teaching their recruits to shoot,
it seems so pointless. One of our captains went
fishing in the river Lys, the last time we were in
billets, with a collapsible rod ; he caught nothing,
but there are said to be fish there, of the baser
sort. There's not much news to spin out a letter ;
perhaps I shall have more to say when we get back
into billets.

Trenches : March 23, 1915.

Writing is difficult, for Sonia, the trench cat, is paddling about on my knees, and making herself into a living sporran. She has come from the ruined farm behind, I suppose, but she takes the change very philosophically, and is a sort of permanent housekeeper, who never leaves company headquarters in this dug-out, but is handed over to each relieving regiment, along with other fixtures, appearing in the official indent. after the ammunition—spades, fascines, R.E. material, &c.—as ' Cat and box 1.' She has no real affections, but prefers kilts, because they give more accommodation in the lap than breeches ; on the other hand, she has an unpleasant habit of using bare knees as a ladder to reach the desired spot. We go back into billets to-night, to a different billet again, I believe, another farm ; it is always a long business getting everything packed up and handed over in the dark, when there is no room in the trench for incomers, and everyone wants to talk at once. I'm not surprised that drifting mines have done such damage in the Dardanelles ; do you remember how we saw the current swirling like a river just opposite the point at the narrowest part ? There was a Turkish pasha, who came on board just before, with his three wives in a small boat, who, owing to the wind

F 2

and the current, were about half an hour in getting alongside, till their silk yashmaks were all drenched with spray, and the pasha, who had come by an earlier boat, was quite concerned, not for them, but for his small boy. I think those long silk veils must be most unpleasant to wear. How the Greeks used to laugh and shout, if the wind blew them up, as a Turkish lady struggled up the ship's ladder; but, according to Pierre Loti, it doesn't matter so much if anybody sees your face, provided that they never see the back of your neck. I don't know why that should be considered such a dangerous spot, but it was a Greek superstition that devils entered into possession through the ears; and that, I believe, is the reason why a woman covers her head in church, because of the angels who used the same approach, and could not all be trusted. Now, of course, on board ship all the ladies go away and put on Sunday hats before service in the saloon, which makes them more, instead of less, conspicuous, just the last thing St. Paul wanted, as he hoped to keep the attention of his male congregation by leaving nothing for their wandering eyes.

There's a new language growing up in N.E. France which would surprise you—the language in which the British soldier addresses his hostess in billets; its chief phrases are 'so long' and

'nap poo'—I suppose this last was once 'il n'y
a plus,' but now it's used like the Chinese 'no can
do' for everything. You will have as many patients
soon as you can manage, I'm afraid, for the hospitals
will be overflowing ; probably you will get some
A. and S. H. sooner or later, for we send away one
or two wounded men almost every day, and the
91st must be sending far more.

Billets . March 24, 1915

We had a very wet night for our relief, which has
made the clay as slippery as ice again, but to-day
everyone has been drying and cleaning, for we have
only spent three of the last fourteen days in billets,
so that it is time We have changed our billets
again ; I am in one farm here with two platoons ; the
rest of the company is scattered, and we mess in yet
another house, so that there is a great deal of wandering to and fro, hunting for other people. It was too
late to get any food or any water last night, so that
the morning found me very hungry and very dirty ;
but now I have had a hot bath, and got my hair cut
by a very talkative French hairdresser. There is
nothing I hate more at home than a chattering hairdresser, but out here it is rather interesting to hear
what they have to say about the war ; though we are
in France, we see so very little of the French. My

platoon are all sleeping in a loft which they reach up
a hen-ladder ; I hope the floor won't give way, but it
creeks most ominously. I see signs of green on the
hedges now ; as usual the elder tree and the gooseberry bush are the first to open their leaves ; the
magpie is busy with his nest in every row of poplars.
I quite agree with you that we *must* get the Germans
driven out of France and Belgium before we begin
to talk of peace, and we shall do it too, though, of
course, the cost will be very heavy. I wish you were
here in charge of an anti-aircraft gun, for I think
you would enjoy that kind of shooting ; you live up
in billets, with your gun and limber on motor lorries ;
then, when a German aeroplane is signalled, you
rush off, and follow him up and down the roads at
full speed, blazing away at him, so that he gets no
peace to observe, even if he escapes a hit.

Billets · March 25, 1915

I have your letter of Sunday to-day, with its list
of parcels, all of which I think have arrived, except
the parcel of socks for the men, which was not sent
by post. Officers' parcels are fairly safe, but I notice
when the men open their parcels they have often
been broken on the way, and in their letters they
constantly complain that parcels have never reached
them. It's a dirty shame, but it seems to be the rule

out here that the farther a man is from the fighting line, and the less hardship he has, the worse does he behave, and the more does he grumble. Our transport were quite indignant the other night, when we came back from the trenches, at being kept awake after ten P.M., whereas none of us had had a long sleep for five days. This has been a wretched day, very cold, with rain and wind from the north-east. We paraded twice for a route march, but both times the rain sent us back, so I have done nothing except inspect rifles, bayonets, and ammunition—a daily task—and lecture to my N.C.O.'s on the way to read a map. Some of them do not even know how to find the North star ; not that that matters in the least just now, but it might make a lot of difference in a confused night attack ; and in these days you can never be sure that an officer will be left to direct them. We shall have to turn out to-night and march down again towards the trenches to dig for some hours ; rather a hopeless task, for this rain will have made the mud like glue again, and the communication trench, which we were clearing out, is sure to be flooded. We are in the usual farm, with the usual midden in the middle of the court-yard ; there is a big dog there too, chained to his barrel, who is having the feast of his life on scraps of bully beef. All these French farms have a wheel outside, in which the dog runs round and round, pumping water

or working a hand-mill. I could never make out
how the wheel worked at first, for it seems to be a
dog's holiday just now. The old farmer, with whom
I had such a violent argument in our last billet about
cows and horses, gave me a ' hurl ' along the road
to-day ; I was glad to know he bore no malice. He
has a face just like Joseph in any Holy Family by
the old Flemish masters, very honest, but round and
rubicund and ordinary, and he drives about in a
curious conveyance, not much larger than a peram-
bulator with the hood up. I get so used to the
landscape that it's difficult to describe it ; we look
across a mile of ploughed fields to the spires and tall
chimneys of the town   There are ditches and pollard
willows and tall poplars, and the telephone wires
to Brigade Headquarters and the different batteries
run everywhere, on their black and white poles,
and strung from tree to tree. For the guns are all
round about, planted in orchards, or hedges, or
behind sheds, where no one will see the flashes. It's
very difficult to see them even as you pass, and must
be twenty times harder from the air. No one knows
how many there are, for they come and depart like
woodcocks in the night. But there is always some
firing going on ; the smaller shells make a noise
like a loose stone sliding down a scree as they go
through the air, but the bigger ones are more like
a train in the distance. The men call every German

shell a Jack Johnson, but as yet I have had no experience of the real Jack Johnson, the heavy howitzer shell of sixty pounds or more which Tom had every day on the Aisne. In fact, none of us who come out now in the spring will ever know what those autumn and winter months were like, when we were always fighting against heavy odds, both in men and guns ; and there are few enough left to tell , but it is those men and their traditions who have really won at Neuve Chapelle, and will win again in these coming months. When I see these long lists of names, I like to think that they are more recruits for the greatest army of all, which is worth far more to the men still fighting here, than any reinforcements in flesh and blood ; an army which is above all the chances of war, and never comes up too late. I hope we reservists and men of the new army have the same spirit ; if we haven't, neither three nor thirty millions of us are much use.

Billets . March 27, 1915.

I'm glad to think that you are at Rhuveag, for you lost your holiday last autumn, and it is a long time since you were away. . . . I am sending you some photos which Tyson took at the base ; they are on a very small scale, and not very clear, but they will give you an idea of our wintry weather there. A month has not made much difference in temperature, for there have been snow showers to-day—how often have we had to shelter from them behind a stone dyke when fishing in Easter holidays!—but this keen north wind is drying up the ground again. We had a short route march this morning, with one piper for the company. It's difficult to get along the roads, the strip of firm ground, or *pavé*, is so narrow; then on either side is a yard or two of hopeless mud, and then a deep slimy ditch; and, of course, supply wagons, artillery horses, A.S.C., and odds and ends from various regiments are all trying to get along at the same time. Most of the infantry now wear the soft 'Gor'bli'me' hat which looks horrid, but does not give such a mark as the flat-topped 'Brodrick.' Then I have been practising with my revolver, and then had a cross-country walk with Tyson, past a lot of ramshackle, picturesque old farms, with the British soldier in his shirt sleeves to complete the picture. The soil here is extra-ordinary—I have never seen a stone yet—and it must give tremendous crops. All the farmers are ploughing and sowing as usual, and, strange to say, they all seem to have plenty of fine strong horses. I should have thought that the Germans would have taken them all, or, failing that, the French military authorities; but here they still are, as if there was no firing line a mile and a half away. Yesterday afternoon I went into the town, to a theatre ! The 2nd Division keep a troop of Follies, who perform daily, with two French girls to help them. They are really very good, songs and stories, step-dancing and so on for a couple of hours. The male performers are of course soldiers, but I think they are struck off their other duties, and certainly they deserve to be, for they do good work in keeping everybody cheerful. All leave here is stopped at present, but this third corps is still very quiet. You get so used to thinking of 400 yards as a considerable advance that it is strange to think that a man could walk the whole length of the British front in one day. I wish I could get the chance to do it. All cameras have to be sent home now, so I'm afraid I shall get no more photos. If they would only trust you to take nothing which could do any harm, you might get a lot of interesting things. I suppose the daffodils at Rhuveag are not out yet, but I hope you will have sunshine.

Billets · March 28, 1915

I had your p.c. this morning, written just before leaving for Rhuveag, also the pamphlets ; as you supposed, prophecies don't interest me very much, but I shall hand them over to the men to-morrow

ın the trenches ; the other two I have not had time
to read yet. We go back into the same trenches
to-nıght ; it's very cold still, but dry, and that
makes all the difference. This morning I had a walk
instead of going to church parade, along the banks
of the river Lys ; it was a marvcllously clear day ;
all the red-tiled roofs of the farms were shining in
the sun, and I could just see a hill in the far distance
with a chapel on the top of it. There is really
nothing to stop you from walking for 20 mıles,
except the fear that an order to reinforce the
trenches might possibly come in your absence.
Being Palm Sunday, the French people were carrying
about sprays of something green ; it looked like
box. I see that many of the khaki scarves which
Sister Susıe knitted are now adornıng *Sœur*
Suzanne ; also all the little French boys are wearıng
khaki puttees ; and I think every French famıly
in the north of France has been living on British
jam and ' boulıbif.' I am sendıng home a *Wykehamist* ; there have been a great many in the lists
lately whom I knew at Winchester. I heard a
good deal about the earlier fighting last night from
an officer in this battalıon who came out in August
as a private in the Scots Guards, and before the
end of January had got a D.C.M., a D.S.O , and a
commission ; he had also commanded hıs regiment
for thırteen days—rather an amazing career ; now

he finds this part of the line unbearably quiet, and
no wonder, after what he describes of Ypres and
La Bassee. Well, this is a short letter, but we are
all packing up again, and just remembering all the
things we meant to do this time in billets. Much
love.

Trenches · March 29, 1915.

This war makes one realise more and more that
men are not good enough yet for universal peace ;
pacificists tell you that 'man should not add
unnecessarily to the suffering of man' ; when he
has learnt not to do it in his daily life, he may be
able to refrain from doing it in war, but not till
then. It was very cold indeed last night, moonlight glinting on the frozen pools, and at 4.30, as
the dawn came up, there was that curious effect
of daylight fighting with moonlight, which makes
everything look so weird. To-day there is glorious
sunshine ; one of those days when the light seems
definitely white, and even the sky is dazzling to
the eyes. We are very comfortable again in the
same bit of trench ; Sonia the cat is still here.
The guns have been busy this afternoon, and the
Germans have given us a few bursts of shrapnel,
but otherwise there is no change. I am starting
to read 'The Mill on the Floss,' the third time I

have started it, I think ; this time I shall finish it.
Have also read Prof. Cramb's lectures on Germany.
I think a lot of what he says about the Germans
is very true—some of them have a sort of idea
that they will first conquer the world, and then
impose upon it the blessings of German thought,
and a new religion which has shaken off the mistaken Christian ideas about charity, and love,
and mercy for the weak. That is one sect ; and
there is another which believes that it would
be a kindness to this poor distracted world to
introduce Prussian system and method into it.
Fortunately, the thing can't be done.

Trenches : March 30, 1915.

I got the nasturtium seeds last night, but the
nights are so very cold just now, that I shall just
wait to put them in. We have bright sunshine
all day, but the ice is thick in all the abandoned
flooded trenches in the shade. They suddenly
began to shell us last night, and stopped equally
suddenly when our guns replied. It's rather a fine
sight at night ; first there is the flash of the guns,
then the wicked whistling of the shells, usually
three or four in a bunch together, and another
flash as they explode, and then the patter of the
bullets and lumps of earth. But unless the shrapnel

happens to catch working parties in the open, it's very harmless. I read Christabel Pankhurst's speech, which I thought good, and part of Prof. Mackail's lecture about Russia, though I think one learns very little from the appreciation of a whole nation compressed into twenty pages; it's apt to be a hurried catalogue of names, and I think one of Tolstoi's short stories will teach you more about Russia. There must be something very attractive about the Russian peasant, and Russia must have such vast reservoirs of energy still untapped. Whenever I get a chance to travel, I want to go there.

I have just been crawling up the communication trench to the orchard which lies behind us; the trees are in no hurry to bud, but the grass is growing very long and green There are some scattered graves there, as there are everywhere up and down the roads and footpaths. I think the French people will look after them, but many of course are nameless, and unmarked. Here is another photo, one of Bankier's, and if I can get prints, he has some very good ones of men in the trenches. An order came round that all cameras were to be sent home; just after they had all gone off came a counter-order, to say that they might be kept, to the great annoyance of everyone who had packed and posted his camera. So I think that when you go back,

you might post me our common camera, and if
we are still here, I will see what I can do with it.
I have been learning the ways of the machine-guns;
they seem to use them more and more in this war,
and it gives me something to do in the day.
April 1 is the anniversary of Bismarck's birthday,
so perhaps the Germans will make a special effort
then; they seem almost superstitious about these
festivals, like the Kaiser's birthday, and the great
days of 1870.

Trenches: March 31, 1915.

Really there is no news at all, except that our
trench cat is going to have kittens, and that is more
interesting to the cat than to anybody else. I have
just been lying in the orchard behind, trying to
make a sketch of one of the old farms, very un-
successful, but I send it, for it may give you some
idea of what shell-fire can do. No troops have
occupied the farm for a long time, for it had been
well wrecked in October; but about Christmas
time the Germans fetched up a thing called a
Minen Werfer, a kind of trench mortar which throws
600 lb. of gun cotton. They made a target of
the farm—there are huge holes all round about, full
of water, deep enough to drown a man—and I
believe the noise was terrible. Now the walls are

loopholed, and all the entrances and windows
sandbagged, so that we could still make a stand
there, if we were driven from our trenches. The
courtyard inside is all strewn with wreckage—broken
wagons, wheels, scraps of clothing, tiles from the
roof—yet it must have been such a fine old farm,
with a carved and panelled dining-room, and a
moat almost all round it. A kingfisher flew up
the moat as I lay beside it this afternoon, so that
I expect there are fish in it. I found a hollow in
the ground where I could wriggle along through
the orchard, out of view of the sniper. There are a
lot of cherry trees which look as if they would
blossom before very long, and it was nice to get
away from our muddy trench, and lie on clean
grass in the sun ; no flowers yet except daisies and
celandines Almost all the trees have had branches
broken off by shells or bullets, but the tree under
which I lay was a walnut, so perhaps the breaking
will serve instead of a beating, and do it all the
good in the world. An aeroplane went over very
early this morning before it was light, dropping
coloured lights as it went. I expect it was one of
our own, off to raid some railway station or supply
depôt at daybreak. The nights are so clear while
this full moon lasts that I expect they can steer
by night almost as well as by day. Your first
postcard from Rhuveag came yesterday, and I

G

was glad to hear of the sunshine. I can imagine how pretty the loch will be looking, for snow always makes the hills seem higher. Here the only hill is a low ridge about two miles in front. We were on it for a few days in October. Then a French cyclist battalion suddenly jumped on their bikes and rode away without telling anyone, leaving our flank exposed; so we retreated, thinking it was only a temporary retirement till supports came up, and we have been looking at that ridge for four months now without getting any nearer to it. Their big guns are all in shelter behind it; I think they have at least four separate lines, all heavily wired. To-night when it gets dark, I shall have a planting of nasturtiums; the men have found a potato pit just behind which gives them great joy; they cook potatoes all day and all night. Much love.

Trenches : April 2, 1915

We should have been relieved to-day, but plans are changed again, and we shall be here at least three days longer; however, nobody minds that very much if it still keeps sunny and dry. I have been out in the orchard again, and have started a garden with a clump of sweet violets which I found growing on the bank of an old flooded trench. Two blue things caught my eye together—one was the clump of violets, the other was what appeared to be a whole German shrapnel shell—so I jumped across the trench, and immediately fell into water up to my waist ; however, I got the violets, and also the shell, which turned out to be only half the casing, and now I have got the violets planted in it and set outside the dug-out, and this pleases the Jocks very much. The whole orchard is full of splinters of shell. I picked up the fuse of one yesterday which I will post home to you. In fact, the place reminds me of what I used to read about the Château of Hougoumont at Waterloo—the same shattered fruit trees and blackened loop-holed walls, with raw bullet marks in the bricks, and gashes showing white on the branches—only I never thought I should see such a place myself, and perhaps I shall yet have to defend it.

Bismarck's birthday passed off very quietly indeed—perhaps even the Germans are not so fond of ' blood and iron ' as they were—but I hear that their heavy guns shelled our old billets away behind us, without doing any damage. One of the forward observing officers of the artillery lives in the trench beside us and messes with us—different officers come down, but the one I like best is a ranker, and a very smart fellow and quite young too. I know they have promoted a great many since the war began, and quite right too, for I don't believe you

G 2

can manufacture a gunnery expert very easily or quickly.

Mother's letter last night, posted on the 29th, made me see Rhuveag very vividly, as it looks in early spring.

Now that the weather is warmer the government issue of rum is to be stopped! That, as you can imagine, is a bitter disappointment to all ' the boys of the old brigade,' and the empty rum jars are now set about the trenches adorned with crosses ' in loving memory.' But in dry weather every-one is in better spirits; the different trenches get names—Cowgate, Gallowgate and so forth—and there is a notice up prohibiting fishing in the ditch which divides us from the next company. Artists and clay modellers also appear.

The Germans put up a large notice one night, ' Come on, boys, we're ready for you,' but one of our men crawled out after dark and brought it in successfully. They also draw the snipers by putting a turnip on the parapet with a Glengarry bonnet on it !

Trenches : April 4, 1915.

We are to be relieved this evening, though I think it unlikely that we shall have a full five days' rest. Everything is still very quiet here, except for a little shrapnel at breakfast time. It was a very wet night, and the soil is such that an hour's rain makes the mud as slippery as ever, but this is a fine growing day, and the trees will soon be in leaf. It will make it easier to conceal operations from the aeroplanes. That, however, is rather against us, for here, at any rate, we hardly ever see a German plane, though there are plenty of our own.

I am writing from an orchard, to which I have escaped again ; a pair of wood pigeons are busy with their nest in the fork of one of the trees. I hope a stray bullet will not put an end to their nursery, for they must have plenty near enough to them.

The rum issue is stopped now that the weather is warmer ; a good thing too, I think, for some of the men thought of nothing else from morning to night. I was amused by an old Irishman in my platoon, who wrote, ' Give the minister my compliments, and tell him to stik to his flok, and I will stik to mine, but if the elders wish to dish out hot tea to the troops, let them come out to the firing line and do it.'

The Germans are now reported by prisoners to have rows of iron bottles behind their lines, in places, full of asphyxiating gas ; they will wait for a favourable wind, and then pioneers with special respirators will open them ; we are in no danger here, for we are too far away, and I don't expect they will be very successful in any case ; but I need hardly say that the inventor has been promoted. They send over rifle grenades occasionally, bombs on a brass rod, fired from an old rifle ; they make a hellish noise, very suddenly, for you can't hear them coming, but they do very little damage.

I hope you will send out that camera, so that I can take some photos before they change the rule again.

I had quite forgotten this was Easter Sunday—there is little enough to remind you of it here—but I hope you had dry roads for your drive to Callander.

Billets · April 5, 1915.

The whole day, from morning to night, it has rained steadily ; it doesn't matter so much now that we are back in billets, but it makes it very difficult to get the walking to which I had been looking forward I have an upstairs room in a small house, to which I climb by a staircase as steep as a hen-ladder, but for once I have a bed to sleep on, a rare luxury. All the officers are messing together this time, in the usual long dining-room of a big farm-house. I like these old farms ; they are well designed to shelter man and beast, both in patriarchal numbers, and the rooms are well proportioned. But, unfortunately, the present generation paints the wooden panelling, and then pastes a cheap wallpaper on top of that. There are two or three glass cases protecting dusty, dingy bunches of artificial flowers ; a wonderful thermometer and barometer combined, which gives you the temperature Réaumur and Centigrade, neither of which scales mean anything to me till I have translated them laboriously into Fahrenheit ; however, the thermometers also record the correct heat for ' bains ' and for ' chambres des invalides,' as well as the degrees of cold at Lille in 1738, and other invaluable records of the kind. Then there are various pious prints on the walls, coloured and terrible, and framed certificates of the family's first communions, *souvenirs précieux à bon chrétien*, side by side with portraits of deceased bishops. This part of France is still very Catholic ; every room has a crucifix in it. Perhaps though, the enlarged photographs on the walls are most characteristic—they are very well done—typical of the French farmers and their wives, solid, sober people ; a little mean and suspicious of strangers at first, but honest and imperturbable. Both in face and character they are utterly unlike the traditional Frenchman as he is known in England ; still more unlike the popular idea of the French woman. But they make it easier to understand how France has been and remains a great country, whatever a Paris mob may do in a revolution. Of course the middle and southern France must be quite different, they supply the new ideas and enthusiasms, and these northerns bring the pendulum back again ; that, at least, is how I imagine it. I have been for a walk in pouring rain with Tyson ; very little to see, for the clouds were low, and there were only muddy horses and men on the roads, and farms usually with shell-holes in their roofs. But they will soon mend everything when the war is over, and if I were a Frenchman, I should feel as if I was scoring off the Boches by running up a new house, planting new trees in the orchards, and filling up the pits where the shells have burst. That part of the damage of war seems so easily repaired. Some kind friend has sent me a pocket Homer this morning. I don't know who it is, but it is a pleasant thing to have in one's pocket. At the moment, of course, it seems absurd to be able to read Greek at sight but not German. Still, it is my own fault that I can't read both ; newspaper articles I can just manage ; they always seem to me just the same in any language. We are sitting in a very hot smoky room, with a gramophone going all the time, so I will finish this rather professorial letter.

Billets : April 6, 1915.

I have actually been to a new place to-day, a village about five miles off, to which I marched

100 men for baths. It was a nice, fresh, sunny morning, and we had a piper to bring the French women and children to their doors to see us pass. Mud and muddy khaki everywhere, paved roads, poplars, and the usual square farms, with the evil smelling moats round about them. Some of them are regular fortresses, with gatehouses guarding the only way in, and narrow slits of windows hanging over the water; but, of course, a brick wall is worse than paper against modern artillery; it doesn't keep the shells out, and it makes more splinters when they burst. The baths were in a factory for bleaching and printing cotton, great wooden vats, in which, I suppose, they soaked the stuff or boiled the dyes. Now it is a Rest Depôt for the 6th Division, full of Red Cross stores and ambulances. We had to keep the men well under cover, in case of aeroplanes, but they enjoyed their baths; and I had one too. We picked up a very large lame dog there, who insisted on coming the whole five miles back with us, in spite of a very sore foot; some of the men might learn by his example. There was a most forlorn row of graves there, in among the factory buildings, just a few wooden crosses outside a drying shed. Somehow it seemed a very comfortless place to put them. But out here you see very much more clearly that it really does not matter a bit what happens to a man's body,

and I think perhaps all the ceremony of a funeral gives it too much importance. These wooden crosses will not stand the weather long, and now I believe the government are to send out iron crosses in their place ; very different from the Kaiser's, but perhaps better earned. The road was bristling with sentries outside all the different billets, rather a nuisance, for it means calling the men to attention every time you pass them, and giving ' eyes right ' or ' left.' The Staff, too, in their motors are a great trouble to the humble infantry. I got a sniff of bog-myrtle from your letter this morning.

Billets : April 7, 1915.

This has been another rather wet day, and I have done nothing except go for a short march in the morning, and a short walk this evening The rain had cleared off, and there was a fine sunset in a stormy sky, which lit up miles and miles of country. We are on a slight ridge here, so that we can see the German ridge plainly about three miles away, and the trenches are in between. Everything was washed very clean after the rain, and the new corn is sprouting very fast in these endless, flat, ploughed fields. I notice that they are breaking up a lot of grass this year, which has been untouched

for years; high prices for wheat have done that,
I suppose, or else the lack of stock. I know that
there are twenty-three dead cows in one field behind
our lines, a problem for the sanitary authorities,
since no one can get near them to bury them. I
passed by one rather attractive house, not half a
mile from here. I suppose it would have been
called a *château,* for it stands surrounded by a
moat, a long building of two stories, with rows of
high French windows, and a sort of terraced garden
behind the moat, on to which the row of lower
windows opened. There is only one entrance across
the moat, a high white gateway, with a crucifix
let into the gable above the keystone of the arch.
Behind was an older house, now a farm, also
surrounded with a moat, with a high peaked roof,
and a little belfry. There was a large cross in white
tiles let into the red-tiled roof; many of the farms
have these crosses on their eastern side; that is,
the side the shells come from, so there often is a
great hole through them The *château* itself was
wrecked, for it stands just behind the village, of
which I'm sending you some photos; please keep
them carefully. Even the orchard was full of great
scars, where the shells had broken up the turf,
and many of the trees had been purposely cut
through, and then held in their places by wires.
So that, if we ever found it necessary to fall back,

they might be swept away in a moment to clear a field of fire from the *château* windows and the trenches beside it   I know nothing at all about Kitchener's army, much less probably than you do at home.   But I have seen guns which will give Ally-man an Easter egg some fine morning big enough to surprise him.   We go into the trenches again to-morrow night   I think the men prefer it now in fine weather, and I shouldn't mind either, if I could get more exercise.

Trenches . April 9, 1915.

'   We are back in the place where I got my first introduction to the trenches, but I would hardly recognise it now, for a month's work has altered it entirely.   The breastwork is finished, and we are no longer holding islands in the old flooded trenches in front.   I have a very respectable house too, with a raised bed of planks and straw, and we can move about in cover where we please, even by daytime.   All the same, I would rather be in our last trenches.   Our heavy batteries have been very busy to-day, but that doesn't really concern us in the firing line, for they drop their shells two or three miles beyond us.   The sniping for some reason is very much less, in fact last night there was hardly a shot, and their machine-guns were silent. To-day we have had fierce hailstorms at intervals, great blue-black clouds driving up all of a sudden, just as they do in Scotland every April. But though they make the surface sticky, the water is steadily sinking. I forgot to tell you that in our last trenches one man spotted a hare sitting in a field behind us ; he knocked it over at 130 yards and in an hour it was soup. . . . I lost my field-glasses last night, but they were picked up in the mud later. It's very odd that they should have unstrapped their leather case, but since they have come back, I must just assume that they managed it.

Trenches : April 10, 1915.

The last twenty-four hours have really been a blank—the usual rounds at night, visiting sentries, the usual slipping and stumbling over abandoned trenches and mud-holes in the dark, the usual stand to arms at daybreak, and then sleep.

The Germans are still very quiet opposite, except for search-lights and star-shells at night—they bring up the search-light on a motor wagon, I think; at any rate, it appears in very different places It's still cold and showery, but the hedges are getting greener steadily, and soon the trees will begin too. We have only wide muddy fields behind us here, so that there's no attraction in wandering about by day.

I, too, have been thinking of other Easter holidays, especially of Florence as I saw it in spring, and Athens. Spring in these southern countries is delightful—for you have the excitement of seeing new people and places, as well as a new clothing for the country. And I liked Torhousemuir very much too, and can remember very well the night when I cried myself to sleep. You were asking why it was—and it's a strange coincidence that you should ask me now, and that I should write and tell you from the trenches. Someone had been talking about what I was going to be, and it was suggested that I should be a soldier, but you said that ' Bey would never be a soldier, for he was not that sort,' and I took it as a great insult—but you were quite right, for it's not really a profession which suits me very well, though I am very glad to be an amateur soldier now. No doubt the reason why children enjoy themselves so much is that they feel things so intensely, and throw themselves completely into whatever they are doing. I always approve very much of the place at the beginning of the ' Inferno,' where the people who had the medieval vice of ' acedia ' were stung with wasps and hornets as a punishment because they didn't really care about anything. Here are Gwen's letters;

she has never had a touch of that vice, and that is why everyone likes her so much

Trenches : April 12, 1915.

To-day we have been sitting outside our dug-outs basking in the sun like flies, and there has been a big hatch of March-browns which has made me think of fishing. It was very quiet too, so that I think the Frenchman might have said again, as he said of the charge of the Light Brigade, ' C'est magnifique, mais ce n'est pas la guerre,' especially when the French are fighting so hard away to the south, and having a Neuve Chapelle almost every day, without shouting so much about it. . . .

We should be relieved again to-morrow night, and go back into billets ; hare-stalking is the only sport in the trenches ; I have not gone in for it yet, but one fellow has bagged two with his revolver ; rather rough on the hares perhaps, for they are all playing about in couples. Send me a few yards of fishing-line, and some small single hooks ; I'm sure I shall find some kind of fish in the moats round these farmhouses ; at any rate, I can fish in hope, and if you can get me a pocket microscope, it would be a toy for the trenches when there is so little to do. I wish we could hear some more news from the Dardanelles.

Trenches : April 13, 1915

We have some more Territorials in the trenches with us for instruction. I never saw a happier kind of school-treat. They had a nice mild night, dry, and not too dark, so that they could avoid the pitfalls. I think they would all have liked to be sentries, or go out for patrols in front of the wire ; this morning they were all squibbing off their rifles, just for the pleasure of writing home to say they had had a shot at a German, and they were far too excited to go to sleep. Their enthusiasm will soon wear off, I'm afraid, but it's quite refreshing to see it. Several divisions of them have come out lately, and I think they will do very well, for they are all very keen, and a good stamp of man, better even than the new army, I should think. The camera came last night, a very neat present, and I shall try to get some photos with it before I have to send it home. . . . But I don't expect to get any very startling pictures, for I have no experience with these small films, and there is nothing very exciting to snap just here at present.

We are to be relieved to-night, and go back to the same billets, I believe, where we shall have a full mess again ; subalterns keep on arriving, some from the Artists' Rifles out here, so that if Sholto doesn't get out soon, he may have to wait till the ranks are thinned again ; now that the dry weather is coming, many of those who went home sick in winter will turn up again, and many of the wounded must have recovered now too. . . .

I see a gleam of sun, so I shall get out the camera. I have just taken one of my bomb-thrower, with a long-handled bomb, and a most ferocious expression ; he's a funny old Irishman, who used to be in the Camerons out at Tientsin, and now his brother in the Black Watch has got a D C.M., and he is very keen to do the same. Our heavy guns have just been blowing some houses to pieces behind the German lines ; it was high time, for I know they used to snipe us from the windows, and keep machine-guns there. It's quite windless, and it makes one think of tennis.

Billets : April 14, 1915.

Did we spend your birthday in Athens four years ago ? or was it on the way to Constantinople ? I'm sorry Venizelos could not persuade the King of Greece to join us, but I think very likely Greece may come in yet, possibly without a King, but with Venizelos president. We are back in billets again, the same billets, and I have had a bath this morning, and must spend this afternoon waiting about while the other subalterns in the company go and do

H

likewise. The town was looking as deserted as
usual, except for khaki. . . . All the men want
their photographs taken, so that they may send
them home, and they pose with bombs in their
hands, and rifles at their shoulders, so that the
friends may be terrified, and suitably impressed.
The trees and hedges are getting greener every day,
but it is rather a cold late spring, it seems to me,
seeing that we are as far south as the south of England, and in the ' charmant pays de France ' I have
just been into a house where some of my men are
billeted, and seen an old woman, who looks like a
witch, making a decoction of black currant twigs
over the fire ; I wonder what she is going to use
them for. I did a great deal of solemn saluting
this morning, with French postmen and policemen.
There is something very comic about French officials ;
for instance, a notice just outside this house, ' Regle-
mentation concernant les Pigeons voyageurs,' which
insists that they shall be provided with ' bagues de
naissance ' on their legs. I got a copy of the *Matin*
to-day ; very little in it, except another instalment of
their serial, ' La fille du Bosche,' which I always
enjoy. Well, next year we shall have to have a
wonderful birthday party to make up for all this.
I think we shall be home by Christmas time, but
I don't think very much before that, unless for a few
days' leave.

Billets : April 15, 1915.

Well, I narrowly escaped a court-martial last night, for in the evening , after dinner, I walked back to our field ambulance station, a mile and a half away, with the doctor, who was going to inquire about some cases he had sent down to hospital Luckily I had told Clark I was going, for, as luck had it, there was an alarm of sorts before I got back, and everyone tumbled out and stood to arms, expecting to move off at any minute. It was only a test alarm, I think, to see if we were ready, but things would have been very unpleasant for me if they had moved before I got back. As it was, I enjoyed the walk very much under brilliant stars, very peaceful, hardly a sound of war ; but, of course, you can see the star-shells up and down the line in the distance, and the beams of the German search-lights sweeping across the sky. The doctor is a Cambridge man, and a very clever lung specialist, I believe, when he is at home. To-day was real spring, without any nip in the air, for the first time , there was a heavy morning mist when I started off for a route march, but it soon blew off the ploughed land. We only went about four miles, for we can't go far from the brigade area. In the afternoon I had just to be a loafer, for others were going to bath and ride , but I escaped again in the evening to my old ruined château, where

H 2

I noted one or two places for the camera, but the sun was too low last night to let me try them then. There are some peach and plum trees in blossom, but the main orchard is not so far advanced. There are, at any rate, fish the size of sticklebacks in the moat, for I have seen them, so there may be something larger.

A German aeroplane appeared in the distance during the day, so all the footballers lay flat and still, while the anti-aircraft gun gave it a few rounds, and it disappeared. We are always afraid that it might occur to them to shell this row of houses. Earlier in the day I watched a battery of our own field guns firing. You see the flash, and a puff of bright green smoke, and then the whole gun recoils more than a yard on its spring mountings, and slips into position again. It looks so very quiet and easy till you hear the roar, which is not, of course, till a second or two afterwards These small field guns make a big noise, especially if you are more or less in front of them , the howitzers give a bigger vibration and rattle the doors and windows, but since their muzzle is pointing higher, they don't seem to crack in your ear as the others do. Everyone is talking of making a cricket pitch. I have finished this letter in bed, morning of the 16th, and there is every promise of a fine warm day.

Billets : April 17, 1915.

This was a quiet day along the front of the 19th Brigade, without any 'substantial progress' or 'notable advance' to record, but I suppose we may say we have 'maintained and consolidated our position.' It amuses me to notice how Sir J. French has refused persistently to publish reports unless it pleases him. Parliament extracted from him a reluctant promise that he would publish a bulletin twice a week, but when he can't be bothered to send anything, he just says he will send none, as there is nothing to report. As you will see from his dispatch about Neuve Chapelle, some of our generals have not done all that was expected of them ; no blame to the man personally, for no doubt he does his best, but a general gets so much credit when things go well that he must take the blame too. I spent the morning throwing dummy bombs with my platoon ; that is most important in these days, for it's the only way of clearing these deep German trenches, when you get hold of a piece of them It's curious how this war has brought back into use many devices which were thought obsolete—mortars, for instance, of Crimean pattern ; breastworks instead of trenches, also a Crimean trick ; grenades and grenadiers ; and though I always thought jackboots absurdly big and heavy, I now see that I might have known, that

Marlborough and his men knew what it was to go through a campaign in Flemish mud ; soon, I believe, we shall have something very like the Roman catapult for slinging bombs from trench to trench ; it has the advantage over every kind of powder that it makes no noise, and so you can't switch a battery on to it and knock it out. This afternoon we spent at a thirty yards range, doing musketry practice ; curious to be shooting at cardboard targets when there are living ones only a mile and a half away I am just off with a digging party, and shan't be in till midnight, so good-night.

Billets . April 18, 1915

My letters lately have been rather short and dull, I'm afraid ; when I have seen anything new, or have anything interesting to say, I can write, no matter what is going on beside me, but when, as always happens nowadays, I have to spin a letter out of nothing, it's impossible to write properly in the mess, and my bedroom hasn't got a table. However, this morning I have escaped to a sunny bank in the orchard just outside our old headquarters farm. There's just a little breeze, but hardly a cloud in the sky, so that daisies, dandelions, and celandines are all wide-eyed to the sun, and the buds on the cherry trees will not be able to keep shut much longer.

I didn't write at all yesterday, for I had a couple of other letters overdue, and in the evening we had a concert. It was rather a curious scene ; they laid down faggots in rows on the midden in the court-yard, so that the men might sit there, along with the hens, cows, pigs, and horses, and they stood round three sides of the yard too, leaning against the walls under the eaves. Then on the fourth side, which was rather a higher platform, there was a piano, a space for the artistes, and chairs for the officers. It was not a very good concert, for the piano could hardly be persuaded to make any sounds at all, and no one quite knew whether they might cheer or clap as loud as they liked, in case somehow the Germans should get to know, and drop a shell among us ; but it was a beautiful clear night, with a very young moon hanging in the branches of a tree just above the steep barn roof. Clark sang, and I think the men would have liked to give him a rousing welcome, for he is very popular, and his new ribbon for his military cross has just appeared, but, as I say, everyone was shy of shouting too loud ; the voices sounded rather thin in the open air, as they always do, but I think everyone enjoyed it in spite of the cold, and there must have been five hundred men sitting there in rows. . . .

This morning I walked over to Church of England service in the yard of a very old farm, which you reached through a gatehouse and a bridge over a moat, but the chaplain was almost too jocular and familiar. I believe that's a mistake even for the men, for they can quite understand a man who is serious, and don't expect a chaplain to smack them on the back, during service at any rate. To-night we are for the trenches again, B company in reserve, all except one platoon, which is mine, so that I, like Uzziah, am for the forefront, though not, I hope, for the same reasons, and I don't suspect anyone of King David's motives. However, I shall have an interesting place on the flank of the battalion, joining on to the next brigade a bit of our line which I have not seen before. I must try and get some photos. . . .

Trenches : April 20, 1915.

We have rather a strenuous time at present, so that I did not write yesterday. It's not that there is much firing, for, on the whole, we are very quiet. But there is a new trench and breastwork in this particular corner which needs to be finished, so that we are kept busy most of the day and night, digging, filling sand-bags, putting up hurdles and piling earth between them, setting barb wire along the front, and carrying sacks full of bricks for paving the muddy places in the bottom of the

trench   But there always remains the morning
from 4.30 till 2 for sleep, so that there's no real
hardship in working the rest of the day.

My flank rests on a railway across which we
cannot build a breastwork, for it is always shelled,
so we have to tunnel underneath, and then we
get down into the water, which complicates things ;
but the weather is dry, and yesterday there was
sunshine, and a windless, cloudless sky from dawn
till sunset.   There is another orchard behind, where
the trees have been severely pruned by shell-fire,
and a lot of ruined houses from which we fetch the
bricks , also we have a stream of running water,
which is a rarity in this countryside, though, running
as it does from the Boches to us, I don't trust its
waters to be so fresh as they look.   They used to
send bottles down it with messages in them, but
that was in the days following the Christmas truce
when the Saxons were opposite.   I rather think
we have Saxons against us now, but there are
Bavarians not very far away, and they have a
reputation as bad as the Prussians.   The Saxons
shoot very little, and are always shouting across.
We have a fine mess-room, plenty of space to stand
upright.   But when we were sitting there last
night, there was a sudden sh-sh-sh and a shell burst
just in front, so near that flying pieces or lumps of
earth pattered on the roof.   You forget all about

the guns until you hear them, but at any minute, if the batteries on both sides chose to fire in earnest, they could make this spot unhappy for the infantry.

I got your clipping of Lord Rosebery's speech on Dr. Chalmers. . . . There seems to have been something about Dr. Chalmers which, more than anything he actually *did*, made a tremendous impression on all the men of his time.

We had a couple of shells beside us to-day, but they did no damage. It's a most beautiful spring evening, with all the birds singing very clearly from the pear trees in the orchard behind us. The fish-hooks have come, but I have no chance to use them just at present.

Trenches : April 21, 1915.

We are still enjoying dry trenches and dry feet, and in a little while we shall have it all paved with bricks, so that, even if the weather does turn wet, it will never be so bad again. The aeroplanes, too, have been enjoying the clear windless weather, and when they get busy the guns get busy too. We were shelled twice to-day, but not more than a dozen shells altogether, and no damage done. This was rather lucky, for two burst between my fire trench and reserve trench, in the space of about

fifteen yards, and riddled the sand-bags which my
men had just been filling before the first whistle
sent them under cover   You can usually hear these
shells coming in time to get out of the open.   They
are not very heavy, only field guns, I think, but
one of my men got a fine brass nosecap from
one, which he is polishing as a souvenir.   There has
been very heavy cannonading all day and all night
away to the north lately; we shall no doubt hear
presently what it is all about.   It's a good distance
away, for we can only just hear the guns, but the
northern sky is lit up with their flashes at night.
The colonel, adjutant, and padre all came to lunch in
the trenches to-day, so we gave them a great feast—
roast chicken from tins, spinach, gooseberry pudding,
cheese, beer, cocoa, and liqueurs—and they had two
shells for dessert and excitement, so that I think
they were quite sorry to go away.   We do not
always live quite so well in the trenches, but still
we all eat far too much, because there is so little else
to do.   I took some photos—one along the railway
line toward the German trenches—which I hope will
come out, for I just held it up on the parapet above
my head, and snapped without putting my head up
to see the view-finder.   It's a very neat little camera,
and I shall be very sorry to have to send it back.
As I write the sky is full of little puffs of fleecy smoke,
where the anti-aircraft gun is chasing the aeroplanes ;

they hardly ever seem to get very near, but they are said to have improved vastly in their shooting since the war started, and even a few shells somewhere near must make it far more difficult to observe accurately. Tyson has gone down the line with fever, or a feverish chill, so I don't suppose I shall see him again, and I shall miss him, for he, too, liked a walk, and preferred a walk to the tea-shop in the town. No word yet of Kitchener's Army in the field; I hear that we have taken a German position to the north, and that repeated counter-attacks and bombardments on their part have failed. These successes may not be very big, but they have a great effect, taken together, on the spirit of our troops, and also on the Germans. We shall be in May directly; time passes very quickly out here, or, rather, there is nothing particular to mark it, so that, although it seems a very long time since I left Sunderland, very little seems to have happened in the space between. . . .

Trenches : April 22, 1915.

We still have April sunshine, so that, in spite of the cold winds and frosty nights, the hawthorn hedges are quite green, and the desolate cabbages in among our barbed wire are sprouting vigorously. We have leeks there too, and every night a party goes out to gather them, so that at all hours of the day and night there is a fragrant smell of frying leek from various odd corners. We have been working hard day and night at these trenches since we came in, and they are a great deal better now than when we found them, but there is still plenty to do before we can think of flower gardens just here. Our airmen were very busy again to-day; they take very little notice of the German shrapnel, but just circle round and round like great hawks. However, the Germans fired so many shells at them to-day that the pieces began to come down all round us, and if I had taken two sizes larger in boots, I should have had a shrapnel bullet in my toe As it is, I have it in my pocket, and will send it home when we get into billets again to-morrow. . . . This would be splendid weather for walking, but I have been digging lately for exercise, and don't feel quite such a slug as I was a week ago. . . . I wish I had had a camera at Bedford, and also at the base camp, for it would have been so interesting to have the pictures afterwards, but somehow I was too much occupied at Bedford to think of it. The men have started playing quoits with the round plates which divide the layers of bullets inside the case of a shrapnel shell; there are a good many lying about, and it makes quite a a good game for them when they are well under cover behind a breastwork. . . .

Billets : April 24, 1915.

Your letter arrived an hour ago ; also the parcel with the writing-pad, which I am now using, and the cigarettes, one of which I am now smoking, and the magnifying glass. I'm afraid I keep you very busy sending parcels, as if I was having a series of birthdays ; but I wish you would anticipate my real birthday and send me a new Burberry, lined, for I have torn my old one all to rags on barbed wires, rivetting hurdles, tumbling over things in the dark, and I think that if we do move I shall drop my great-coat and take a lined Burberry instead. No, we were not at Hill 60 ; the work there was done by Tom's old Division, the 5th, and especially by the K.O.S.B.'s and the R. West Kents, who charged the hill with the bayonet after our mines exploded, and then held to it all night. How he would have enjoyed that if he had been there ! Sir Charles Fergusson, who now commands the Second Army Corps, has been highly praised, and especially the 13th Brigade; but probably you will know all this before you get my letter. When they got to the crest of the hill, they found that it was used as an artillery observing post by the Germans, who had massed forty-five batteries in preparation for an attack on the 28th of this month, unknown to us ; so we just took them in time. I learnt this from the forward observing officer of our batteries in the trenches yesterday. Of course, all these forty-five batteries turned on to the hill at once, which accounts for the tremendous bombardment which had been going on at intervals night and day for the last five days, and they must have given our troops a devilish hot time of it ; all you read in the official report is that ' we consolidated our position through the night in spite of a heavy bombardment,' which means that officers and men would be digging like niggers while heaven and earth were dissolving in fragments all round them, and whole platoons getting blown into space by heavy shells, for you can't hope for much cover on the crest of a hill. For that reason, too, it will be very difficult to hold the hill now that we have taken it, but even if we were to lose it now it would have been well worth it ; but for that I suppose our front line of trenches would have suffered the fate of the Germans at Neuve Chapelle on the morning of the 28th.

The Germans have been bombarding Ypres again, too, with 42 c.m —15-in. howitzers—and did a lot of damage to houses, and the artillery generally has been rather active, and is blazing away as I write.

Yesterday, about 5.30 P.M., a German 4·2 howitzer dropped two shells plumb into my trench, but for some extraordinary reason only gave one corporal a small scratch in the hand ; one man's pack, which he had taken off, was riddled, and another man had about six holes through his canteen. Another corporal standing a few yards from me got a piece of shell plumb on the breastbone, but it only bruised him very slightly ; and yet three days before a flying piece from the same kind of shell hit a steel rail on the railway beside us and shivered a yard of it to splinters, which shows what queer things shells are. The men dug up the nose-pieces of several of them, solid caps of brass and copper weighing two or three pounds ; they were so keen to keep them that I did not like to claim them, but they would have made fine ink-pots And no wonder the Germans are running short of copper if they use so much of it in one shell ; most of them were dated 1915, and one had the fine old German name of Simson on it. I think they were really just registering the range on that bit of trench because it was newly made, but certainly they got the range to a T. The shelling kept me busy at the time when I should have been writing to you, but otherwise I never miss a day. . . . We were relieved safely last night, and marched back into billets, and so far as I know we only lost one man wounded these last five days, which is less than the battalion has lost in any spell of trench work since I came out. We have a communication trench now across the fields behind, which makes it a great deal safer ; before that they had a nasty habit of turning their machine-guns on to the roads about 8 P M., and hunting the roads with their search-lights. I really enjoyed this last spell in the trenches, but it is always nice to get back into billets, after sleeping in one's clothes and boots for five days and nights. For at night we have to sleep, when we lie down at all, in our equipment too, which means that you wake up with the butt of your revolver digging into your ribs, and your kilt somewhere round your neck It doesn't matter so much when you go to bed at one A.M., and stand to arms at 3.15, for then we sleep in the morning with boots on but equipment off. However, last night I revelled in my Jaeger sleeping-bag again, and went to sleep in a pleasant smell of plum-cake, from Mother's last shirt in the parcel, which was wrapped round the cake. I never care to look to see how dirty I am at night, for it's hopeless to start washing then, and too late to start hunting if the coverts have to be drawn. But this morning I walked in to the bath again, and I'm glad to say that I haven't been much troubled with the Scots Greys, as the men call them.

I'm afraid that many of the stories about killing our wounded are quite true. The 3rd Corps publish a sheet of news every day, which is circulated all round the different regiments, and a few days ago it contained an extract, dated back to December, from the diary of a German officer

I

captured by the French. He said : ' The scenes in
the trenches and the fury, not to say bestiality, of
our men beating the wounded English to death
made me quite incapable of attending to my work
for the rest of the day ' At Neuve Chapelle, too,
some horrible things happened, when German
prisoners, who, in the confusion, were left insuffi-
ciently guarded, turned on their escort.

I don't think our men would ever do that sort
of thing, though I can quite imagine that, if they
had charged across the open and through the barbed
wire, under heavy fire all the time, they might not
be inclined to take prisoners the Germans who put
their hands up at the last minute, after doing as
much damage as they could ; but I don't think they
would ever bayonet the wounded   I remember the
first time I was in the trenches that, when I came
out from my dug-out one morning, a corporal reported to me that they had seen a German working
in the broad daylight in front of the German wire.
I asked if they had fired on him, and they said
no, because they thought he must have been sent
to work there as a punishment, so they wouldn't
shoot him   Yet the Germans won't even allow our
stretcher parties to work.   It's impossible to prevent
ignorant soldiers from getting out of hand occasionally, when there are no officers to watch them, but
what I hate is the thought that these devilish

cruelties are encouraged by German regimental officers, and even by their General Staff, as a deliberate system of war. . . . Would you send out a set of rope quoits for the men to play with? We can fix up pegs for ourselves. . . .

Billets : April 25, 1915.

We have had a very quiet Sunday ; the cannonade to the north seems to have stopped at last. It was unfortunate that the French on our flank there had to give way ; but perhaps the line has now been recovered again, and this war is a game on such a vast scale, that you never know whether what seems a loss may not be a deliberate move to draw away attention from some other move elsewhere. I have done nothing but read and write, and potter round our billets ; it has been a sunny, cold evening, such as I often remember at the beginning of cloister time at Winchester, when enthusiasts in sweaters tried to persuade themselves that the cricketing season had really begun. It's really much too fine to be fighting, it seemed more appropriate in cold miserable weather ; but the latest German trick of letting loose poisonous gas on a vast scale makes one feel less and less scrupulous about fighting them to the bitter end There never can be any real peace in Europe while one nation is convinced that *anything* which can possibly gain it an advantage in war is morally right. Fortunately, I think a lot of these ingenious tricks will recoil on the inventors ; if you train soldiers to depend on all sorts of mechanical assistance, they will be lost when the time comes to depend on themselves alone. Anyway, these stories make me lose all regret, except the personal one, for lives lost on our side in this war ; they are necessary sacrifices for the lives of all the rest, and for finer principles. Some men, like young Gladstone, are fortunate because they can give a name as well as a life for the cause they believe in. I can't think who the A. J. R. is in that clipping you sent me from the *Spectator*, James Fort's little poem ; the *Wykehamist* isn't published in the holidays, so I haven't had any news from Winchester for a long time. . . . They are coming to lay the tables for dinner, and there is no more news, real or imaginary, to give you.

Billets : April 25, 1915

We have a perfect sunny day, with a gentle north wind which still brought the distant sound of heavy firing this morning It has been a big fight near Ypres, and will be bigger yet perhaps. . . .

I had a long conversation to-day with a Belgian hairdresser ; he said that before the war Belgium

was bitterly divided between the Flemings speaking
Flemish, and the Walloons, who spoke French, for
the Flemings were supposed to be German in sym-
pathies; but now both parties hate the Germans so
much that they are welded into one. He was of
the opinion that men must always fight something,
and would be fighting in strike riots if they weren't
at war. Perhaps he's right.

We are going to have a rugger match to-morrow
against the Cameronians; one way of getting fit ...

Billets : April 27, 1915

I was down at the range all this morning trying
to improve the shooting of the worst shots. I think
most of our men shoot remarkably well, but there
are always one or two who let down the average.
We had something very like an easterly haar, but
it cleared off to a hot sunny afternoon, far too hot,
in fact, for our rugger match with the Cameronians,
which we lost by three points to nil; the dress of
the players was varied and peculiar; for instance,
a canary coloured sweater and a pair of thin sky-
blue shorts; one player, in fact, had got such a dia-
phanous garment that he had to pin a striped towel
round his waist when it was seen that there were
French girls in the crowd. However, the game was
furious and bloody, and the men enjoyed watching

it, and shouting the result, like newspaper boys, when it was all over. There were welcome intervals, as, for instance, when the ball went into an evil-smelling moat beside the farm, and had to be retrieved with poles. I shall be very stiff and sore to-morrow when we go back to the trenches

We are still waiting to hear the result of this furious fighting in the north, but I think it will probably last for several days yet. Here we are peaceful as usual, and so long as we don't move from here, you really need not be anxious, for we have not had an officer hit for over six weeks. I don't want to alarm you by talking about shells and bullets in my letters, but it is no use pretending that they don't come along occasionally, for, after all, this is war, even in the trenches when there is no attack in progress.

We had another concert last night, and since some officer had to be the victim ' pour encourager les autres,' I had to face the manure heap in which the audience were sitting and sing them the Skye boat song, which can't often have been sung in a stranger place; really one needs a voice like a bull to sing in the open air without any accompaniment. The favourite songs are sentimental, e.g. ' I lost the sunshine and roses when I lost you.' We are all beginning to get sunburnt, and everyone is looking and feeling far better since the fine weather set in; also there are not nearly so many ' drunks,' for stricter measures have been taken to watch the French *estaminets*.

I don't see any end to the war yet; a good deal will depend on what happens in this battle up north; if we could give the Germans a really hard knock, it would have a tremendous effect, for their losses at Hill 60 must have been appalling; they always are in an attack which fails. . . .

When you send out my photos, keep the films but number them, so that I can order any more prints that I want, and send out several prints of any that are good, for all the men are sure to want to send them home; they are promising them in their letters already, so I hope they have come out well. . . .

Billets · April 28, 1915.

This has been a really hot day, and makes us wonder what it will be like in July. Everyone is getting that slanting mark on the forehead by which you can tell an officer in a Scotch regiment, where the Glengarry makes a dividing line between sunburn and white skin.

I have been making a bonfire of old letters, for, though I am keeping some of yours, the others were accumulating very much, and it's always difficult to get rid of them, for I never want to burn the whole lot, and one must read them all over first. The Germans were shelling a village some distance away with heavy shells ; you saw the smoke first of all, and then heard the whistle of the shells—black smoke when they just hit the ground, red smoke when they burst on brick houses, which took a beautiful salmon-pink colour in the sun as it floated away. The Frenchmen in the fields went on ploughing and harrowing as usual. I am going to share a big dug-out with Clark this time and we ought to be very comfortable, with an upper and a lower berth to sleep in . . . .

Trenches : April 29, 1915.

I wonder if you have such a perfect evening as we have here ; the sun has really been very hot, everyone in shirt sleeves complaining of the heat, as if we had quite forgotten already what it was to be wet and cold. I am back in a trench not far from where I was last time ; the pear blossom and cherry blossom is really very pretty, and we have cuckoo pint coming up among the grass. There are minnows in the stream too ; they always seem to appear with the first really warm day, as if they were born from the mud ; but they will have to get used to soapy water this year, for a wash in running water is not too common, and the men appreciate it.

I have got hold of a book of Tolstoi's stories. There's something very charming about them, they are so direct and simple; and in the same book one has sketches of Sevastopol during the seige, curious reading just now, when we are doing our best to give the Russians what we fought to prevent them getting sixty years ago. I once read them before in French, and I think I'm right in saying that he doesn't mention the British once—it's always the French, and yet we all have the habit of thinking that we did all the fighting in the Crimea. Some time we must all go to the Caucasus, as we used to talk of doing, for a summer shooting

I think this expedition to the Dardanelles is intensely interesting, a great risk but a great prize if we succeed; and what a difference it would make if all the wheat now lying useless in Southern Russia could be brought out. You remember all those empty tramps steaming up the Bosphorus, high out of the water, to get their cargoes of wheat as soon as the ice broke up.

You remember that sonnet I sent you a few weeks ago. Well, I see that Rupert Brooke is already dead, at Lemnos, from the effects of sunstroke; he was in the R.N. Division, so his wish has soon been answered.

You will be walking about the lawns at Hopetoun, playing golf with the patients, I hope. You must be learning a lot about different kinds of men, for I think men from the ranks show their differences more on the surface. Public schools leave men just as different underneath, but they make them more alike in small things and externals, so that it takes longer to make a guess at them when they are on their guard.

By the way, the sight of bare arms passing makes me wonder why tattooing is so popular; almost every soldier seems to be tattooed somewhere, especially soldiers who have been to India. I can't say I ever wanted to be tattooed myself, but I suppose there is some attraction in it.

Trenches : April 30, 1915.

I don't know whether this letter will go off to-night, for the colonel came along at my epistolary hour, and then there were several knotty points about separation allowances. They plague us perpetually about them even here ; none of the officers know what to do, and the men don't know either ; their wives and dependants complain that

they aren't getting all their money, and the regulations have been changed so often, that there is
no firm ground to go upon. However, I think I
must try to master the subject; in fact, I should
have done it before. We have had another extraordinarily hot day. Now that the pear blossom is
fully out, I notice how black it makes the branches
look, and if I were a Japanese painter, and had a
large sheet of blue paper to represent the sky, I
could make a study in blue and white and black;
in writing, that only suggests advertisements of
Stephen's blue-black ink; but it's really very
pretty, when all you see above the trench is the
sky with a black and white branch of blossom
in it.

I'm still eating too much, and taking too little
exercise, and now that we have the sun to bask
in, it's even easier to sit and do nothing, for what
work remains to be done can hardly be attempted
by daylight. I have started to read ' Richard
Feverel ' again; perhaps I should be reading and
rereading military text-books, but this war is so
utterly different from every other war that sometimes it seems very little use, and I must rest my
poor civilian brain sometimes. . . . I was very
glad as usual to get your Sunday letter last night,
and the centre of *my* world's interest is where you
all are, so don't imagine that the smallest things
don't interest me.

Trenches : May 1, 1915.

We have had yet another day of sunshine, but there was more of a breeze ; yesterday it was so still that the puffs of smoke from the air-craft guns just stayed still in the air, until they gradually melted away. I was on duty all last night, so I saw the merry month of May come in from its very beginning, a soft, mild night and a full moon, very pleasant for walking up and down in the hollow behind the trench and thinking of you all and of Gwen in Nairobi. It's a great thing to live in the open country and the open air, day and night, as we do in the trenches. I enjoy that, and wonder how I shall be able to settle down to an indoor life in a big town when this is all over. . . .

I read the pamphlet, it was quite good ; but just occasionally I seemed to hear the 'voice of the preacher,' and though I hope this will be the last war for a long time, I don't believe that it is the last war of all ; people are not ready yet to feel themselves citizens of the world, rather than of their own country ; there was a time when they were content to be subject to a foreign government, because they were only interested in their own small city or county, but for the last two hundred years the feeling of nationality has been growing stronger and stronger ; you see that in the history of Italy, and of Germany especially ; and I don't think we have reached the end of that period yet, for the Eastern countries are only just beginning to share that feeling with the West

I must read Lloyd George's speech   The *Daily Mail* accuses him of not having a sufficiently high opinion of the working man, which is rather comic when you think what the *Daily Mail* has said of Lloyd George in the past.   I wish every public-house in the country could be run on the same lines as those of the public-house Trust down in Surrey and thereabouts : the system under which the manager gets no bonus on alcoholic drinks, but does get one on everything else.   The result is that any man who wants it can still get his beer or whisky, but it's to the manager's own interest to make the 'general refreshments' as attractive as possible.   That's a more natural way of working than total prohibition ; but I'm for taking whatever measures the government think necessary *for the war* ; nothing matters compared with success in that.   Heavy firing to the south this morning ; the K.O S.B. seem to have lost most of their few remaining officers ; all regiments have suffered heavily, but none more so than they.

Trenches : May 2, 1915.

I have had a pretty long day, beginning at 3.15, but quite a pleasant one. Some officer in the company has to stay awake in the morning hours, in case anything should happen, or a German aeroplane come over within rifle-range. It was my turn to-day, not a very sunny morning, but grey and mild. I watered our garden ; the pansies and forget-me-nots are growing well ; the other plants are not so happy after their transplanting, and the Middlesex, being townsmen, do not seem to understand about gardens, and when they water the plants at all, they do it at midday, under a blazing sun. I found a nest full of young hedge-sparrows too beside the stream which runs through our breastwork, and saw the very father of all the water beetles at the bottom. Remembering how hard these large water beetles can bite, I left him severely alone. There were some British aeroplanes, but no Germans, and what with newspapers and a new book, I soon found it was 5 o'clock and breakfast time. The book was a new one about Belgium, in the Home University series, written by a Wykehamist called Ensor. If you want to know something about the Belgians, in a conveniently packed form, he's your man. I'm ashamed to say that, until this war, my two main ideas about

the Belgians were that they ran at Waterloo, and
that they were responsible for the state of the
Congo, neither of which is very true. . . . I thought
Lloyd George's speech in introducing his Bill for
dealing with the drink problem very courageous,
and the mass of evidence overwhelming, to show
that something stringent must be done. . . . Even
a small number of drunkards can do an infinite
amount of harm, and the good have got to suffer
for the bad in a crisis like this. It's just the same
out here ; most of my men are good honest fellows,
whom I should be proud to lead, but one went
sick this morning because he had taken cresol, the
disinfectant, undiluted, and deliberately poured it
into his boots, so that it might inflame a scratch
on his ankle, and send him to hospital. He was
determined to get out of the trenches somehow
That type of man makes discipline severe, because
you can't deal with him gently, and it's the same
with drunken slackers at home, even if their numbers
are small in proportion to the whole. But it will
be difficult to deal with the thing properly, for it
will naturally be unpopular with the working men ;
and, besides that, there is the enormous strength
of the liquor trade, which will raise the familiar
cry for the poor widow, who has put her money
into a brewery What Lloyd George said was very
true, that ' people agreed about the facts, until

they came to consider the remedies, and then they altered the facts to suit their opinion of the remedies,' and began to say that there was no unusual drinking after all. . . . It would be cheaper to pay wages and dividends for every brewery and distillery in the kingdom than to prolong the war for one unnecessary month. These next two months will be critical; the risk at the Dardanelles is very great, but so will be the reward if we succeed, and out here the trial of strength will come home to everyone. There has been tremendous firing, as heavy as I have heard yet, to the north all this afternoon. We shall hear about it presently. . . . When I spoke about the workmen, perhaps I wasn't allowing enough for the craving which seems to seize on some men. But even if they are to be more pitied than hated, we must protect ourselves against them, if we want to end this war quickly.

Well, to-morrow night I hope we shall find ourselves back in billets; it seems odd to be sitting here so quietly in the sun, watering our forget-me-nots, within sound of all that desperate fighting.

Trenches : May 3, 1915:

We go back into billets again to-night, but it has been so warm and dry and comfortable that this spell in the trenches has seemed the shortest of any since I came out. We have not heard yet the meaning of all the firing to the north last night; though I believe the Germans made another attempt to attack, with the help of their gas-pipes, at Hill 60. But the rumours which I hear is that the wind changed, and caused the gas to hang about the German trenches; our guns then turned on to them, and smashed their iron bottles and apparatus, so that they were obliged to leave their own first line of trenches in broad daylight, pursued by our own shrapnel, and suffocated by their own gas. I hope it's true, but they stand to lose in any case by their use of that gas; they lose the good opinion of every neutral country, and of the best men in their own. And in any case they can only use it in exceptionally favourable circumstances, which they can't expect to have very often. We have all got respirators now, gauze pads, and flannel gags, twelve pairs of goggles to each platoon, and bottles of sodium bicarbonate, which combines with chlorine, I think, to make it into harmless salt! So that if we breathe through pads soaked in that, we shall be safe, but very thirsty! No doubt they will go on using the poisonous shells, which are easier to manage. The Canadian Eye-witness' account of the fighting was fine reading, and should make them very proud in Canada; they must have fought splendidly, and so, of course,

K

did the British troops who came up to relieve them;
but the battle's not over yet. I was glad the Eye-
witness paid such a fine compliment to the French;
we are always apt to think that our own men
wouldn't have lost so much ground, but we can't
possibly know that, and all we do know is that the
French felt the full effects of the gas-cloud. . . .

Just up into billets. I have your letter and
mother's. Thank you for taking so much trouble
with the prints.

Billets: May 4, 1915

The three parcels of socks have arrived, but I
have just given orders to put them into the battalion
store of socks, and then those who need them most
will get them. My own platoon has had about a
dozen odd pairs from me, and there is no use giving
too many, for they will just throw them away,
instead of troubling themselves to wash them or
darn them. This sounds very wasteful, but it's just
what all men, including myself, will do when there
are no women to scold them for it. I also have a
cake, the new Burberry, and the parcel of quoits,
all of which make me feel that I am being spoilt; but
thank you very much for them. This is a fine hot
day, with thunder in the distance. I have escaped
from the mess and my bedroom to the garden of a

deserted villa. It has been put in a state of defence; the garden wall is loop-holed, and there are trenches and sand-bag parapets running through the flower-beds; notwithstanding, it is still very pretty, pear trees and cherry trees in full blossom, and the apple trees too are beginning to show their pink, while the flowers are putting up a good fight against the weeds. I will get you a sprig of lilac presently, when I have finished writing, and I hope a photo which I have just taken will be a success. I'm glad the others were good, and the men were very pleased with the copies that I gave them, but there is a great demand for more. . . . My rest in billets is being disturbed, for I have got to take my platoon back to the reserve breastworks to-night—only for one night, though. This is a new idea of the brigadier's. They shelled our billets at lunch time to-day, but without doing any damage. I was sitting by the window in the mess, when there was a sudden whistle and a 'crump' in a cabbage patch about thirty yards away, and there were half a dozen more round about. It was a little uncomfortable while it lasted, but everyone continued to read the news-papers and smoke with affected indifference. These Territorials up at Ypres have had a very rough baptism, for I don't think they had been out more than a few days. But it was lucky for us that we anticipated the Germans at Hill 60, otherwise they would have pinched the angle at Ypres from both sides, and very likely would have taken the town.

Billets : May 5, 1915.

This day began for me about midnight, as I lay in my dug-out in the breastwork watching the plough swing slowly round. I shall remember that night ; there was a heavy thunder-shower in the evening, but when we marched down it cleared away for a warm still summer night ; still, that is, except for the sniper's rifles, and the rattle of the machine-guns, and sometimes the boom of a big gun far away, coming so long after the flash that you had almost forgotten to expect it. The breastwork which we held ran through an orchard and along some hedge-rows. There was a sweet smell of wet earth and wet grass after the rain, and since I could not sleep, I wandered about among the ghostly cherry trees all in white, and watched the star-shells rising and falling to north and south Presently a misty moon came up, and a nightingale began to sing. I have only heard him once before, in the day-time, near Farly Mount, at Winchester ; but, of course, I knew him at once, and it was strange to stand there and listen, for the song seemed to come all the more sweetly and clearly in the quiet intervals between

the bursts of firing. There was something infinitely
sweet and sad about it, as if the countryside were
singing gently to itself, in the midst of all our noise
and confusion and muddy work; so that you felt
the nightingale's song was the only real thing which
would remain when all the rest was long past and
forgotten. It is such an old song too, handed on
from nightingale to nightingale through the summer
nights of so many innumerable years. . . . So I
stood there, and thought of all the men and women
who had listened to that song, just as for the first
few weeks after Tom was killed I found myself
thinking perpetually of all the men who had been
killed in battle—Hector and Achilles and all the
heroes of long ago, who were once so strong and
active, and now are so quiet. Gradually the night
wore on, until day began to break, and I could see
clearly the daisies and buttercups in the long grass
about my feet. Then I gathered my platoon together, and marched back past the silent farms
to our billets. There was a beautiful sunrise, and
I went to sleep content. Then I walked into the
town to get a bath; it was a hot May day, sunny and
steamy, and the garden of the house where we get
our baths has two fine tulip trees in it. Then on the
way back I went round to the 24th Brigade Headquarters to ask for Roger Hog, and found him there
looking very big and healthy. He is telephone

officer, I think, and very happy mending breakages, and inventing new devices, and his colonel and the other officer were very pleasant. He walked back with me part of the way, and you can tell his mother when you see her that her son is 'in the pink,' as my men always say in their letters. The afternoon I spent in getting plants from a ruined village for our trench gardens—wallflowers, pæonies, pansies, and many others ; rather cruel to transplant them perhaps, but there are plenty left. The village is a terrible sight, for what the shells have left standing has been wrecked in the search for wood, for burning and making dug-outs in the cold wet weather last winter, and you notice the contrast more now that the fruit trees are all in blossom, and the garden beds have all their spring flowers. There were many books lying about in the wreckage on the floors, mostly Catholic Lives of the Saints and other books of devotion, but I saw one Greek grammar. There was a school too, with its windows all broken, and great jagged gaps in the walls where the shells had come bursting through ; so that there was a touch of grim irony in the inscription on the walls—

Le Don de nos Benefacteurs,
Enfants, prions pour eux.

There are graves, too, everywhere in the little gardens behind the houses, and except for the birds and an

occasional soldier passing, the place is very quiet.
One old couple still live in their house, I believe,
because they have nowhere else to go. . . .

Billets . May 6, 1915.

Here are some photos from the Yang-tse which
Harry sent me the other day; you will recognise
some old friends. Someone who was looking at
them yesterday pointed out that the joints in the
forelegs of the kneeling elephants are made to bend
the wrong way. I think the picture of the women
on the terrace among the fruit trees was taken near
that great mound which excited the Canadian so
much, because he said it was 'raised from the dirt of
eighteen provinces.' The journey up the river to
Hankow, and even above that, would be well worth
doing, if one could go there again. Harry is still in
the tropics, but not allowed to say anything about
what he is doing. . . . I have had a letter from Mrs.
Haldane full of the latest instructions and diagrams
for breathing in spite of the gas, but we have all
got respirators now, and bottles of solution in the
trenches, if we have time to use them. Here that
is not likely to be a difficulty, since we are 300 or
400 yards apart, but in places where the trenches
are very close, there is not much time to prepare.
It's so difficult not to make a joke of the whole

thing when we practise breathing through pads &c., but it's no joke when they turn the taps on, and our doctor, who rode over yesterday and saw some of the victims, has come back full of wrath. I hope we shan't be obliged to retaliate with the same weapons, but if we are driven to it, we have the south-west wind in our favour nearly two days out of every three. . . . I spent yesterday afternoon getting plants from a ruined village. In most cases I think they will have to pull the houses right down and start all over again. Some of the deserted gardens are very pretty, and the wallflowers are particularly fine. We shall get vegetables presently, too, green gooseberries, and prickly artichokes. But, as a rule, the French there seem to take very little trouble with their gardens, and it is only accident and the rich soil which makes the flowers grow so well. I have to take a party digging to-night, so I must send this off.

Billets. May 8, 1915.

I have come back to the deserted garden to write to you; four hot days have made a great difference to it. The lilacs were hardly out when I last wrote, but now they are very gay—white lilacs too—and though the pear tree is green instead of white, there is an apple to take its place. Four demoiselles come to the garden, too, to pick the lilac, and both yesterday and to-day we have had long conversations, with a great many gallant compliments on both sides. But you need not be anxious, for their ages are six, five, four, and three respectively, and besides I told them that I only came to the garden to write to my mother, of which they highly approved. I showed them my skian-dhu; they nodded gravely 'c'est pour les Allemands,' then most bloodthirsty gestures, to show me the right way of using it. They jump in and out of the trenches, and carry off great bunches of lilac, so that I think they are thoroughly enjoying the war, and fortunately I had some chocolate in the pocket of my kilt apron. Now that the weather is so fine, it seems most absurd to be fighting; we go back to the trenches again to-night, and in future I suppose we shall have to watch the wind, in case they try the gas here too. We had a practice attack here this morning on a trench which we dug yesterday — wire-cutters, bomb-throwers, sand-bag men; most realistic; so realistic indeed that there were one or two casualties—two sprained ankles, and one man slightly wounded with a piece from a bomb; for unless you practise sometimes with true bombs, the men can never be persuaded to treat it as anything except a joke. They are still fighting away in the north; the failure of the

French to recover the lost ground north of Ypres was certainly most unfortunate for us, but we shall be on our guard against the gas in the future. It's curious how few, comparatively, of the officers in the casualty lists belong to the regular army now; there are so few left. . . . Give my love to J——. I have hardly ever seen her since the leave-out days when Tom and I used to go down to Alverstoke and play golf with her round about the old forts; usually she beat us badly, I think. . . .

Trenches : May 9, 1915.

We are back again in the trenches, all wearing respirators round our necks, and watching the wind, in case the gas should come drifting down; but I don't think they will try it here. There is a lot of fighting going on at different places, and I hope you will hear good news in a day or two How pleased the Germans will be that they have sunk the *Lusitania* ! . . . It's no use protesting against them now, except with the bayonet , their leaders must have lost their heads in their rage, and I think it's a sort of just judgment for their gospel of hate. This has been a beautiful day, much fresher than it has been lately, thanks to a north wind which has still a touch of the sea in it.

The gardens are all flourishing—lily of the valley, pansies, forget-me-nots, and all the old favourites. We are kept busy watering them.

We have all been supplied with Balmoral bonnets, and khaki covers for them; they look hideous, but may be less easily distinguished from the English Tommies' cap over the parapet, and they will perhaps give us a little more shade in July. . . . This is a dull little scrap of a letter.

Trenches. May 10, 1915

We are still quiet here, though there is fighting going on all round us. By the reports the French seem to have done very well down at Arras, and we are particularly glad when they score a success, because the waiting game is more trying to their temperament than to the British troops. That, at any rate, is the usual opinion about the French soldier; but anything more stolid and imperturbable than some of the farmers round here, I can't imagine; they don't look as if they could run, even if they tried. It is a great coup for the German submarines to have sunk the *Lusitania*. . . . We shall have this advantage from the disaster, that there will be no more difficulties about contraband, for every reasonable American will now see that we must fight the Germans with every weapon, and that our interference with neutrals is nothing to what they would have to expect from von Tirpitz loose on the high seas. It just shows how marvellous our navy has been, to lose so little in spite of all their efforts, and it's extraordinary that they have never yet succeeded in sinking a single transport.

I have seen two aeroplanes come down to-day behind the German lines; one of them may have been a German, but the other I'm afraid was British; shrapnel was bursting all round it, and presently it caught fire, and fell down blazing from a great height, so that I'm afraid there is little hope for the pilot and observer. The casualty lists are still very heavy; one begins to look at them to see who's left alive, rather than who's dead; but in these last few days at Ypres, we must have given the Germans a good deal more than they gave us. I had a letter from the Warden yesterday, very indignant at the German barbarities, more especially at the poisoning of wells in German South-West Africa. It just makes one think what an appalling condition Europe would be left in, if Germany won. You would still have the competition in armaments, severer than before, and an endless competition in every kind of devilry when the next war began. For if they succeeded by these methods, everyone else would be forced to copy them . . . We were shelled early this morning ; a bag of coke, sent up for the men's fires, was blown to bits, otherwise no damage was done. Our own guns were busy yesterday, and set a large building on fire, a couple of miles away on the ridge in front of us. When it grew dark, you could see swarms of little black figures silhouetted against the blaze. I suppose it was a storehouse and that they were trying to rescue something. But we telephoned to the guns, and they dropped their first shell right in the middle of them, with several more to follow. After that the fire was allowed to take its own course. ·The wooded ridge looks very pretty, now that the trees are in their first leaf; but knowing the woods are giving cover to the German batteries, we should be better pleased to see the land in front as treeless as Orkney. However, we never give the German aeroplanes a chance to observe accurately now, though our own are circling over their lines every day. It is the hidden machine-gun which makes an infantry advance so desperately difficult ; it's almost impossible to spot them ; they can be hidden in cellars or pits while the position is being bombarded, and then whipped out again before the advancing lines have reached them.

Trenches : May 11, 1915.

There is no use pretending that I am soldiering at the minute, and I don't deserve anybody's sympathy. I'm sitting with my back against a nice comfortable bank of baked earth, my feet have a resting-place just at the right angle on the other side of the trench. The garden is in full flower round about me, and there's a nice breeze to temper the blazing sun. I've had as good a lunch as I ever want to get—curried beef, boiled rice and rhubarb, plum cake, washed down with red wine and soda. There's plenty to read, plenty to smoke, plenty of writing paper. The store-room is well supplied with your last parcel of raisins and figs, and we haven't had a man hit since we came down to the trenches again three days ago. The weather is still perfect ; our trenches and breastworks are brown and bare and dusty, and the sand-bags are getting bleached with sun, but everything else is green. The meadow behind is yellow with buttercups and dandelions ; there's a large patch of yellow mustard out between the lines, and a forest of leeks and cabbages. Even the walnut-trees, which seem to be the last of all, are beginning to give a little shade, and the broken stumps of poplars are doing their best to repair the damage of the shells. I spent part of the morning skittling in the stream, for where an old trench crossed it, some hopeful idiot last autumn had built a dam of bricks, as if that were likely to keep the water out. The remains were still blocking the current and making a stagnant pool, so I cleared them out, to the great disgust of the water beetles and other tenants who had been living there so long. There was a pleasant smell of warm mint and water-weeds, which always remind me of the water meadows at Winchester, and the birds, too, are very much the same. Swallows and house-martins are very busy, but it will puzzle them this year to find a house left with eaves, within a mile of the trenches on either side. Certainly there are none about here, and few walls as high as a second storey. My hedge-sparrows are nearly ready to fly, but I found another nest with young birds, in a pollard willow, a common sparrow's, I think; but there were three bullet holes scored on the bark within a foot of it, so that I did not care to climb up and look inside. The birds don't care, and I often see them crossing between the lines; in fact, there are just too many pigeons crossing, and I wish I had a shot-gun to stop some of them. There was a tit's nest too, as usual in a hole too small for my hand, and too deep for my fingers, so that I must watch for the bird to see what kind it is. This letter has been interrupted by the observing officer for the artillery, who wanted to be shown a place where my sentries had noticed the smoke of German guns ; their batteries are very well hidden, but now they should be able to watch this place, and plaster it with shells when the German guns begin to fire. It's near a church spire, which is doubtless used for observing ; but of course we do the same now when necessary. At the beginning of the war, so Clark tells me, our men would not fire on churches, but they had to learn to do it in self-defence.

Our aeroplanes are very busy again ; it's extraordinarily hard to see them in the sunlight against the sky when they are painted white, or very little yellow ; you can only follow the string of smoke-puffs, and strain your eyes as if you were looking for a lark. When so many shells are bursting up in the air, you would expect a hail of bullets, but somehow the pieces very seldom come down near us. This morning, however, the base of an air-shell came tumbling down, and almost went through the roof of a dugout ; a sheet of corrugated iron saved the sleeper. One of the aeroplanes we saw fall yesterday was a German, the other was British ; but the raids planned by us on various points round Lille seem to have been successful. It must be harder to see troops from the air when the leaf is on the trees ; even the houses which we have seen for months have disappeared, so that you only catch glimpses of red tiles between the branches.

We had a little excitement yesterday at dusk, the stand-to-arms was just finished, and I was sitting down to your letter and my dinner, when a man rushed in to say that a German had crawled up among the trees in front and was throwing bombs. So out we all tumbled, manned the parapet, and started firing. The sentry, who was trembling with excitement, swore that a bomb had hit the ground just in front of him and burst. I hae ma doots. However, presently Bankier went boldly forth for 100 yards in front, to the spot where we have a listening post when it gets dark, and I followed to pick up the bits. But there was no German to be seen, dead or alive, so that, unless he had tumbled into the deep ditch there, he must have crawled away again. It's curious to be out in front of the lines after dark, the place looks so different from that side. There are a couple of solitary graves, beside an old farm road, which comes straggling out of the pear trees in front of us, and wanders away towards the German lines. But the grass is growing thick upon it, for no one could dig up the beetroot last autumn and bring it in ; as for the farm wagon, one of its wheels has been converted into a mounting for a machine-gun, rather a clever little invention, for it just swings

L

round on its own axle, which is buried in the earth, and the gun, sitting on the flat upper side of the wheel, can be tilted and turned to follow an aeroplane at any angle. The war must have come upon these farms very quickly, for almost all the cattle have been killed, and they still trouble us. But a gunner who was here then described to me how he had seen men dash out from their trenches, in spite of the snipers, and run along to cut a steak from the bullocks, and back again. For in these days rations were not so plentiful as they are now, and fresh meat still scarcer.

We were glad to hear to-day that an attack with gas on the 27th Division, in which our 1st Battalion, the 91st, are brigaded, had failed badly. For the respirators saved our men, and the Germans came on carelessly in masses, thinking that they must have gone back, or been suffocated. However, we were all there and ready for them, and they lost very heavily. I think we have scored a great deal already, in spite of the poor victims, by the feeling which this latest German trick has produced. When I censor the men's letters, I notice a different spirit ; they were keen to win before, but they are ten times keener now, and even the faint hearts who said they were 'fed up with the war' see now what they are fighting against. Every battle now will be sterner and fiercer than before, for every man will now be determined more than ever to do his best. We shan't retaliate gas for gas, I hope. . . . I meant to write you a good letter to-day, but there have been constant and maddening interruptions.

Trenches : May 12, 1915.

I have just been looking at a full-page photo in an illustrated weekly with the stirring title, ' How three encountered fifty and prevailed,' and a footnote describing their gallant deeds in detail. The dauntless three belong to this regiment, but we were a little puzzled, because we have never been at La Bassee, where their exploit took place. A closer inspection showed that the trees were in full leaf, and that the men were wearing spats and hose-tops, which we have long since abandoned for general use. Finally, someone recognised the sergeant as our shoemaker sergeant, and his companions as two men from our second line transport. They are usually at least three miles from the trenches, and the whole story is a lie from beginning to end, without a shadow of truth in it. It makes one distrust all newspapers more than ever, to catch them out like that. The photo must have been taken somewhere on the retreat last year. . . . This Division is not likely to get any leave until

L 2

we do some fighting. . . . I'm glad the French have done so well near Arras, and they seem to be still moving. . . .

Trenches : May 13, 1915.

We are going out into billets again to-night; so far the fighting north and south has not changed our routine. This was a day when I could have got a basket of trout, I'm sure ; a nice warm wind from the sou'-west, a dull sky, plenty of flies, and light rain from time to time. But the wind has brought the sound of heavy guns, rumbling and muttering since dawn without a pause. Somebody must be catching it, though we don't know whether it's our own guns or the Germans' which are so busy. But, in any case, this firing, whether or not it leads up to an attack, will help the French to gain still more ground near Arras. Rumour says that our First Army was held up by machine-guns in its attack three days ago. At Neuve Chapelle they thought they had rather overdone the bombardment of the front trenches, and not paid sufficient attention to the strong point behind. This time, therefore, they didn't fire at the front line so long, and in some places the machine-guns hidden at the bottom of the parapet escaped, so that one battalion is said to have found itself up against seventeen of them. But I don't know that there is any more truth in our rumours than in yours which run about at home. The game is so big that we can never see more than a little bit at one time, and when you are playing to a wavering audience of neutral nations, watching their opportunity in every move, even the military moves have all got to be calculated by diplomatists, and arranged to suit their plans too. We hear this afternoon that the French have carried another village, taken six more guns, and over a thousand prisoners. I think that by using gas the Germans have given us a present which will be worth as much as four Army Corps in the field. Nothing since I came out has done so much to rouse the men's spirit; we shall gain far more by these dirty tricks than we lose in lives.

I was sowing seeds yesterday, which had been sent out to another subaltern—marigolds, poppies, and stocks; rather late perhaps, but anyway I hope we shall have moved on long before they flower. What fierce fighting in the Dardanelles, but I hope that with the actual landing, the hardest job of all is over though, of course, there will be a lot of fighting yet.

Billets: May 15, 1915.

Yesterday was a busy day; really we get almost more rest in the trenches now than in billets. I spent all the morning at the rifle range, and then, after inspecting all the platoon's rifles, &c. (the etcetera now includes goggles, respirators, and 'nip bottles' of chemicals), I was told that I had to march a party on church parade to listen to the Bishop of X. I suppose godliness does come before cleanliness, but he made me miss my bath. Until yesterday all I knew about the Bishop of X. was the sad story of the raven in Trinity, Oxford. This venerable bird had lived in the quad for many years, and his tough constitution had brought him safely through a life of miscellaneous feeding, and it is to be feared hard drinking, for he was liberally treated by all his friends. But one fatal day the Bishop of X. came down to stay in Trinity, in a room overlooking the quad, and left the window open when he went out. Some sheets of his sermon blew out into the quad, where they were seized and devoured by the unfortunate bird, who died a few hours later, before he had time to say 'never more.'

Well, anyway, we gathered together some three hundred men, of all persuasions, and marched them off to the Bishop. He came under the wing of the Brigadier-General, or rather the Brigadier was under his wing, for he is a most enormous man. The proceedings began with a hymn, accompanied by a band of mouth-organs, which, unfortunately, tickled my sense of humour so much that I found it hard to keep

my face. Then the Bishop opened his bombardment in that style which seems necessary to bishops
and other clerics in addressing soldiers. When he
wanted to be funny he could be very amusing, and
when he confined himself to his own business, very
impressive. But, personally, I do not care for a
mixture of the two styles, and when a cleric says
' Please God, the Germans will take it in the neck,'
he makes me wriggle in my chair, and feel uncomfortable all down my back. However, as I say, when he
left our German enemies alone, and came to those
others with whom a bishop is more particularly
concerned, he was very good, and I think the men
enjoyed it, for it was something quite new to most
of them.

Billets : May 16, 1915

I enjoyed your long letter two days ago, and I was
very glad to know that Ronald has found some
friends ; but still, of all the men I know, he will find it
hardest to be a prisoner as the months go on. . . . This
has been a warm summer's day, and for me the first
day of rest since I came into billets, for I was busy
with a digging party all yesterday afternoon. It
was only a practice trench, dug in an orchard about
two miles back, for what the adjutant calls ' the
Colonel's new lawn game,' that is practice for attack-

ing trenches. The old farmer was very indignant,
and had spread his very strongest manure on the
grass, in the hope that that would discourage us ;
but we just dug on, while he looked indignant from
a distance. To-day the officers were all photo-
graphed after church parade ; the first group in the
new bonnets, which don't look so smart as the Glengarry, but may give a little more shade. Then I walked
in for a long deferred bath, and had lunch at the
house too ; the garden there is very pretty now with
lilac and magnolias ; it looked so damp and dismal
when I first saw it in March, with high gloomy walls
and dripping evergreens, but now one sees that it
was well designed for shade, which will be needed
presently. The owners of the house have fled to
Paris. But their servants and their dogs, both in
large quantities, still remain, and I think they, the
servants, are quite glad to lay table now and then,
while the dogs, of course, rejoice to see such signs
of normal life returning. There is a very large St.
Bernard, who careers round and round the flower-
beds, while the old housekeeper screams and threatens
in a torrent of abuse and affection. This second
attack of the First Army promises to be more successful than the venture a week ago, but, as you say, one
gets hardened to casualty lists and disasters, for
that is the only way to finish the war. If we are to
have another winter campaign, we shall need con-

scription ; we should have it now, I think, except that the War Office are not ready to deal with such an influx of men. I have got a Russian grammar and a reading-book I can, at any rate, teach myself enough to find the way and ask for food, which are the traveller's first needs I have also a book on botany, which Mrs. Balfour sent. I had written about it to Bay ; he is now attached to the K.O.S.B. at Weymouth, and likely to sail soon for the Dardanelles. . . . It was a beautiful calm evening until our batteries started firing ten minutes ago ; demonstrations again, I suppose, but I hope it will help them to push home their attacks further south. This next fortnight will be important.

Billets : May 18, 1915.

We have had a wet day, and a very wet night. I expect there will be heavy rain here at intervals all through the summer even in June, as Wellington and Blucher found at Waterloo. But it's a great nuisance, because the mud becomes as sticky as glue again at once, and may have hindered the First Army in their advance yesterday. According to the latest reports, they were doing very well, had lost less men than in their attack a week ago ; and what was more important than any gain of ground, the Germans seemed to be surrendering in bunches, as if for the moment, they had lost heart there. Of course we are only at the very beginning of the business still, but it's a hopeful sign. The firing throughout the day was very heavy; they say the gunners get quite dazed and numbed after a bit, so that they find it difficult to pick up new orders or new targets quickly. I can quite believe it. Meanwhile, we were quiet as usual, and I was playing football in the afternoon with my platoon against Bankier's. I think the men enjoy a chance of knocking an officer over for a change. We were just beaten, and, of course, my men blamed the referee, for that's just one of the points where they are like very small boys or children, they can't take a beating, and they do love a grievance. I remember seeing one of the Seaforths at Bedford refuse to take any bread from his friends, so that he might have the pleasure of saying he had had no breakfast. The photos gave great satisfaction; thank you very much for them, and for the compasses. I had a walk yesterday evening when the rain had cleared off; the country is changing very fast now that the leaves have come out, and though at first I thought it very ugly, I begin to like it. There are still many corners where there is nothing to remind you of the war, and then suddenly you turn a corner to find a pile of bricks where once stood a house, or a grave by the roadside, or a great shell-hole, showing up in greater contrast now that the grass is long and green. As one of my men said in writing home about the strikes. ' If them at home seen what we seen here, there would be less talking and more doing.' It's nice to hear of Gwen and her garden. We must be marking time in East Africa at present, waiting until some of our other campaigns are a little further forward. So far old Botha seems to have made as great a success of his as of any ; yet it can't have been at all an easy job.

They are starting to poison water out here now ; a stream running from their lines to ours has been found to be full of arsenic, so we must be careful. No one would have believed such things before the war ; one could hardly believe in them in the Middle Ages. I'll write to Mother this evening before we leave for the trenches.

Billets : May 18, 1915.

This is a cold grey day, with sodden ground under foot, and a grey sky, threatening more rain, just like many days I can remember at Winchester, when even sweaters could not make cricket anything but a miserable game. However, the news of the fighting is still good, and we are gaining ground slowly. I don't know whether this battle will bring it, but some day soon, I'm sure, there will be a sudden and startling change in the whole situation on the Western front. These bloody battles seem to leave things very much where they were, but the Germans are getting weaker every day, and we are getting stronger. You remember Clough's poem—

> Say not the struggle nought availeth,
> The labour and the wounds are vain,
> The enemy faints not, nor faileth,
> And as things have been, they remain,
> If hopes were dupes, fears may be liars—

and so on. The whole of it seems almost to have been written for this long drawn out struggle from Switzerland to the sea. I see Jack Haldane is wounded, but I have no further news of him ; a short time ago he was going round the First Army lecturing on respirators and gas, but I think he must have been back with the Black Watch. The quarterly you sent me is very interesting ; two of the contributors, Gilbert Murray and H. A. L. Fisher, I know well, and Vinogradoff, who writes about Russia, was perhaps the most impressive lecturer I ever heard at Oxford. He was a professor in some branch of law, a man of immense learning, who had really been driven out of Russia because his liberal opinions were suspected by the police. In fact, I think he finally left Moscow University in protest, because detectives were sent to attend his lectures. But now he evidently hopes for more tolerance and freedom as the result of the war. His English was perfect, except for an accent which seemed to give new meaning to the most ordinary words, when he came down upon them with all the weight of an enormous voice, and an enormous body too. . . . I have been asked to write some notes on the doings of the 93rd, for the sake of the future regimental historian. I don't know what is wanted, and it will of course not be easy to make a connected account of what happened before I joined ; but it is as well that someone should try it while memory is fresh, and some of the officers who came out to France with the battalion are still with us. . . . I hope the rhododendrons will be as fine at Rhuveag this year as they were last June. . . .

Trenches · May 20, 1915

These are strenuous days, for the new army has arrived at last, and its officers come swarming down upon us, to see what trenches are like. It's quite refreshing to meet people who are so keen ; we could only with difficulty restrain them from crawling out to the German wire. But it's also a bit of a nuisance, for they sit in our seats and sleep in our beds, and fill up our dug-outs, and, very rightly, ask ten thousand questions which are difficult to answer.

However, we do our best, and they enjoy themselves enormously. I took them along this afternoon to the Buffs' trenches ; they are on our left, in the next brigade. The lines are much closer there, and there are a lot of interesting things. They can't be shelled by the German guns, because the German trenches would suffer too ; but they get a lot of rifle grenades pitched among them, and to protect themselves they have built overhead cover, until their trenches remind you of the lower decks of a ship, with iron loophole plates instead of portholes. Then at one point, where they are only seventy yards apart, they have a catapult, on the Roman or medieval plan—a rack which winds up a cord, and so stretches a dozen strands of the thickest elastic. There is a canvas pouch to hold the bomb, and then you release a catch, and away it goes for seventy or eighty yards, and drops into the Germans. I found a Wykehamist there whom I had not seen for years ; he had been out since the beginning. Finally, the H.L.I. officers hurried off, very pleased with themselves, because they had been out in front last night and the others had not. I took them out with a party of haymakers, for the grass in front is growing so long that we have to cut it to clear our field of fire, and later on they went further out with Clark, and thought they saw six Germans, so their picnic was a great success. To-night a platoon of A. and S. H. is coming in.

Trenches · May 21, 1915.

Writing becomes rather difficult now that the New Army has arrived; we had three the day before yesterday, two yesterday, and two again to-day, and since they are naturally anxious to see as much as possible during their twenty-four hours in the trenches, there are a large number of personally conducted parties, and I am getting quite the guide-book style, when I casually point out to them where a shell burst last week, &c., &c. Of course they ought to know much more about soldiering than I do, for they have had nine months' undisturbed training, with expert advice, and the benefit of any information which the General Staff can collect and pass on to them, whereas in the Special Reserve we were given various jobs, which made regular training impossible—such, for instance, as guarding these two miles of sea-coast near Sunderland—and as soon as either officers or men began to know their work, they were drafted out to the front, and lost to us. They are of very different types; our first three were all as keen as mustard, one of them an Indian officer who had been home on leave when war broke out, and was now a major. Then last night we had a dignified old gentleman who had last fought with the Black Watch at Tel-el-Kebir! He must have been well

over sixty, and had left the army for years, and I
did admire him for coming back, and sticking to
it as a captain, when all his contemporaries were
generals or club critics. But when I took him
round the trenches, I felt rather like a small child
showing its toys to its grandfather, who feels obliged
to take a patient, kindly interest in them. We
tucked him up in Clark's bed at an early hour,
and he asked anxiously whether the nights were
cold, or whether one could sleep with the door
open. . . . I suppose that when he last fought,
it was in a scarlet doublet, with feather bonnet
and sporran and all. To-day one of the men
who turned up had been at New College with me;
he used to write poems quite well, and now looks
quite a smart officer. I don't know what they
mean to do with this division of the New Army,
but rumour says it will be attached to the 3rd Corps.
They shelled us to-day, but only one man was
wounded; another shell went right through the
top of the kitchen beside our mess, where two of
our servants were playing draughts. It put an
end to the game, but nobody was touched, and it
didn't spoil our dinner. . . . I'm sorry that there
should be a political crisis in the Cabinet; the
ground swell after all the storms last year has
threatened to upset them more than once. . . .
I haven't heard what sailors think about the

Dardanelles, but it seems to me fairly obvious that we shouldn't have sent such a large force there, unless it had been necessary to give Russia an opening to the sea. I'm sorry too that we should use gas, and, on the whole, opinion out here, round about my little corner anyway, is against it.

Trenches : May 22, 1915.

There is peace in our lines again, for Kitchener's Army marched off at 2 A.M. before it got too light. Our latest visitors were some of our own 10th Battalion whom we liked very much, and they are said to be one of the smartest in this new division. It is a very hot, steamy, sleepy day, with a hum of bees and flies, which is seldom broken by any firing. There is a smell of May in the air, which reminds me of many happy days in a punt or a canoe up the Cher. This was just the prettiest time of year there, for Eights would have been coming on this week, and I can see Tom very well in a new Leander ribbon and his best blazer, looking very serious before the racing began, and very merry when it was over. The rowing men didn't have much picnicking or punting or lazy sleepy afternoons ; for they were always in training till Eights, and then started practice for Henley after a week's interval. But for six weeks in summer

M

they were the people, and I know how much all Tom's friends in the Eight will be thinking of him now. . . . There must, I'm afraid, be many cripples in spite of modern surgery. But still, if a battle to-day is in some ways more terrible than it was one hundred years ago, it's very much less terrible afterwards, thanks to anæsthetics and research. There's one curious result of censoring so many letters, that everyone is much more apt to make mistakes in spelling from seeing the same words spelt wrong so often. Schoolmasters who have to teach small boys say just the same thing, and I know that when I'm in doubt I always scribble on the blotting-paper, and judge it by the eye. Russian seems to be a language like our own, where words are by no means pronounced as they are spelt, and, like us, they write a great many letters which they never pronounce at all ; I don't think one can go far, without hearing the words pronounced ; just think what a hash a foreigner would make of English if he tried to learn it by book, or how many rules for pronouncing ' ough,' for instance, he would have to pack into his head. The Germans were signalling with a lamp last night ; I pegged out the line of direction on the top of the parapet with bits of stick, just as at a grouse-drive one sometimes marks the line of a bird with an empty cartridge case ; and now by daylight I find they must have been using an old telegraph pole along the railway. I hope you will be off to Rhuveag as soon as this letter reaches you , if thoughts could bring me there, I should not be very far away.

Billets : May 24, 1915

We marched back into billets last night, but after three hours' sleep we were roused up again to stand to arms, in expectation of a fight somewhere near. All is quiet again now and we are dismissed to our beds ; but it is a beautiful clear fresh morning, and I can't get to sleep ; perhaps a heavy meal of plum cake and chocolate at 2 A.M. has something to do with it.

The *Daily Mail* and some other papers seem to be raising a panic cry that our heavy losses in the last few months have been due to the want of the proper kind of shell, and that Kitchener is to blame ; that is not true, and it's a shame to say it. Our gunners can use just as many shells as we can possibly give them, and so can the French gunners and the German gunners, and the gunners of every country now at war. The German batteries are more strictly limited in their rounds than our own in this part of the line, as I know myself from counting the shells sent over. Yet Germany had

M 2

been accumulating a vast stock for years in preparation for this war, and had enormous factories and plants ready. We never contemplated any war of aggression ; last August we had to suddenly start and multiply our army and all its stores by ten. It stands to reason that we can't do in a few months what Germany after years of preparation finds herself unable to do.

The forced retirement of the French at Ypres, owing to the use of gas, let us into a very nasty corner ; the Germans made good use of their advantage, and we lost heavily before we re-established our new line. That's really a side issue. The main point is that for the last three months we have been attacking, in one place or another, lines of fortified positions, which the best brains on the German General Staff, with almost unlimited labour and material at their command, have been preparing and strengthening for six months. That doesn't mean that we can't break their line in the end, we have shown that we can do that ; but it does mean that, shells or no shells, we are bound to lose heavily in doing it. Our artillery may batter their first line of trenches to a bloody pulp, but there are still their second lines and third lines and fortified points to be dealt with. You may knock out nine out of ten machine-guns in position, but the tenth can still

do a lot of damage to advancing infantry, and the
check will give them time to fetch up others from
the rear, or from deep cellars and covered pits,
where no bombardment by any guns will destroy
them all   I don't write these thing to discourage
you, for we can get over all these difficulties in time,
but just to show that we must expect to lose heavily
in the attack, even if the whole front is plastered
with high explosive shells—and neither Kitchener
nor Mr. Asquith nor the Prince of Wales nor the
Lord Provost of Edinburgh can prevent it—nor
yet the *Daily Mail.*   By the way, it's sheer rubbish
to say that shrapnel is useless for clearing gaps in
barbed wire.   Gunners out here will tell you that
it does that far better than high explosive shells,
and daily experience proves it.   It makes me so
angry to see that kind of twaddle in print.   One
newspaper lie more or less is no great matter, but
it is very unkind to all those who are in mourning
to make them think that, but for some tragic blunder,
it might never have happened. . . .

It's a damnable thing to treat this war as so
much material for ' good copy '—as for the photographs of survivors from the *Lusitania*, I can't
imagine what kind of reptile would be mean enough
to creep in front of a woman and snap his camera
in her sorrow-stricken face.   The country needs
a prophet badly, an Isaiah full of white-hot

indignation, to get up and denounce these things, and make us all see that it's not only wrong to print such pictures, but wrong to indulge the morbid curiosity which make us look at them. We should have Dr. Chalmers back again 'to bury his adversary under fragments of burning mountains,' as I think Jeffreys described one of his sermons. However, I'm nearly preaching myself! By way of contrast, do you remember what Mr. Dooley said of the Germans at the time of the Boxer rising, and the punitive expedition? ' 'Twill civilise the Chinaymen,' said Henessy. ' 'Twill civilise thim stiff,' said Mr. Dooley, 'and p'raps it wuddn't be a bad thing f'r the r-rest of the wurrld—maybe contact with the Chinese may civilise the Germans.' But I think I liked best his remark about Christian Science. 'If the Christians had a little more science, and the docthors a little more Christianity, tw'ud make no great difference which ye called in—always pr-r-vided ye had a good nurse.' . . . You seem to have had more east wind than usual; here it comes over miles of land before it reaches us, so that it's often quite a warm wind. . . .

Billets : May 24, 1915.

You and I must both watch the dawn come in very often these days. I didn't get to bed until

daylight for three out of our last five days in trenches,
and last night they roused us in the very early hours,
and I couldn't get to sleep again. However, it
was a beautiful morning, with a ·clear wind, so I
wrote a long letter to Daddy, and then walked in
before breakfast to the house in the town where we go
for our baths. We can get a *petit déjeuner* there—
good French coffee, omelettes, and what is best of all,
a clean tablecloth, and clean knives and forks. The
servants are still living in the house, along with two
terriers, a bulldog, and an enormous St. Bernard ,
there was an even larger dog, but he was killed by
a shell which fell in the garden. It's a very pretty
garden, shut in by high walls, so that it reminds me
of one of those Oxford gardens, tucked away in an
odd corner between the colleges. There is a fine
weeping ash in the middle of the grass, lilac and
wistaria, a couple of beds full of tulips, with tea-
roses soon to follow, and a verandah looking
down the middle, with what I think must be a
niphetos rose—if that is how you spell it—climbing
round the outer side. At the far end there are a
lot of rambler roses which will very soon be out,
and espalier pear trees and vines straggling up a
sunny brick wall, which has a large shell-hole
through the middle of it. But you can't see that
from the verandah ; in fact, you can see nothing at
all to remind you of the war, but only grass and

sun and shade and flowering trees and bushes, and that is why I like it, and the birds all like it too. So I had my breakfast and bath, and came back along a hot dusty mile and more of *pavé*, and found a lot of parcels and a letter from Mother waiting for me when I got back. I meant to write to you yesterday from the trenches, but we moved out suddenly, and there was no time. Two nights ago we had a little expedition towards a single tree which stands among the long grass far over towards the German lines. They had seen Germans working there from the next trenches on our flank, and there was some new earth thrown up. So we determined to see what we could do. Bankier and a fellow from the next brigade crept up to the tree with a supply of bombs, and then Clark took out a covering party to make a diversion on this side, so I went out too. I stayed in a little bit of trench about half-way between the lines, while Clark went further out and further across with an old Irish bomb-thrower from my platoon. It was a still warm night, and we waited there a long time, expecting to hear the bombs go off. There was a low moon, and a great deal of summer lightning, but it was very quiet, except for a little sniping, and the rustling noises in the long grass. I wanted desperately to sneeze, and then the whole thing struck me as so ridiculous that I very nearly laughed out loud.

At last we saw dark figures moving towards us, and sat very still and quiet. But it was only the bomb party, who had been right out and round the tree, and found nothing there at all. So we all filed back again just as it began to get light, and then I could sneeze again to my heart's content. To-night there is a beautiful moon and a cool breeze ; we are sitting up in case we should be wanted, but I don't think that's at all likely. . . . The adjutant has just told us we can lie down, for all is going well, so I'm off to bed, and very sleepy. Good-night.

Billets : May 25, 1915.

We still have glorious weather, and if it is the same at Rhuveag, I expect there will be bathing in the pool under the waterfall which we discovered last year, unless you are still cursed by the east wind. Something big is happening here, I don't know what or where, but it doesn't seem to be near here, although I watched rather a heavy bombardment last night. I believe the 8th Black Watch are not far away, and I wish I could run across Hutchie ; if only they had sent him into our trenches to be instructed ! All your parcels have arrived, I think, so I was able to give six shirts to my platoon this morning, and all the socks ; some men were complaining that they had had no new ones for a long time, and ' the holes soon get big when there are no lassies to mend them.'

The aeroplanes are very busy in the evening hour, for the clear light gives them a chance to observe everything, even from a great height; and there is a great rattle of rifles and machine-guns firing at them, quite ineffectively, I think, for unless an aeroplane has been hit already, and is flying low, I'm sure none of the bullets ever come near it. . . .

My old enemy hay-fever has been threatening me, but the doctor here thinks he can cure it. I hae ma doots o' that, but his mixture certainly does a lot of good.

Billets   May 26, 1915.

This is a baking day, we have just been drilling in our shirt sleeves, and we shall soon need sun helmets if it goes on getting hotter; the nights are beginning to get warm too. It will be useless for fishing if you have the same weather at Rhuveag, but very pleasant for sitting in the sun. The men, too, wish they were home in this fine weather, and I found one the other day writing to his fiancée, and saying that he hoped to be ' roaming in the clover out the Bo'ness road ' before long. Most of them, I think, respect me enough to obey orders, but I don't think many of them like me, for many of them haven't been soldiering long enough to understand

that an officer doesn't give punishment out of spite.
An army which elected its own officers would have
a curious history , it would suffer terrible losses
until it learnt the value of discipline, and then when
the natural leaders had come to the front and made
their own orders, punishments would be far severer
than anything in the King's Regulations. I don't
quite know what effect Italy will have upon the war.
No doubt Italians in Austria were badly treated;
but, of course, the real reason why she has gone to
war is that she sees an opportunity. I don't imagine
that they will be keen to move further towards
Vienna than the boundaries of the Italian-speaking
provinces, but that will always detain a lot of men.
People will scoff at her for waiting so long to make
up her mind, but I suppose her reasons for coming
in are very much the same as ours in the Boer War,
to protect the men of our race who were being ill-
treated in foreign territory. I'll never forget how
rude an Italian was to us in the train leaving Florence,
and how profusely he apologised when he discovered
we were English. He had thought we were Germans,
and he said he made a point of always being rude to
Germans ; as for the Austrians, of course they hate
them for their old supremacy in Northern Italy.

I don't understand yet what is at the bottom
of all the upheaval in home politics. . . .

Billets · May 27, 1915.

I had a letter from you, another from Daisy, and another from Gwen to-day, so I did well. This time Gwen's came direct from Nairobi, date April 27, and I'll send it to you to-morrow. Here we have nothing new, except a very cold north wind. I was amused this morning to see a very fat priest on a bicycle, with his skirts flying in the wind, and to notice that priests wear dress guards on the back wheel. I walked in this afternoon to have another bath, and tried to get a buckle for my kilt in place of one I had lost, but it was difficult to make them understand, even when I took off the apron and let them see for themselves what was wanted. I'm afraid Sholto is not likely to come to this battalion, but rumour says the 91st are moving, and will not be so very far away. . . .

Billets : May 28, 1915.

I go into reserve with Clark to-night, in a farm nearly a mile behind the firing line, so we shall have a rest. The cold east wind which was plaguing you has come to us now, or rather it is north wind here, and comes from the sea, not very far away. Cricket has just begun to invade France, but I don't think it's likely to displace football;

it needs much more elaborate preparations, and would use up an infinite supply of balls in the long grass. We don't seem to be much further on yet at the Dardanelles ; if the Italians could spare a couple of divisions, it would be a great help, but I don't suppose they will send troops out of Italy, except to cross the frontier. This letter was begun last night, but never finished. I don't think I have much more to add to it even after keeping it for twenty-four hours. I have had a very peaceful day, just pottering about this farm, which is close to the orchard where I heard the nightingale three weeks ago. The farm itself is deserted, but there is one 50 yards away still inhabited by a Frenchman and his three little girls, Sophie, Amelie, and Clemence. It's the greatest joke in the world to them when they hear a shell going overhead, and yet the Germans might put one into their kitchen at any minute. . . .

Reserve Farm . May 30, 1915

This Sunday did not begin as a day of rest, for at 5 o'clock this morning I was awakened by a bursting shell. There is no trouble about dressing, so I wandered out across the farmyard just in time to see a shell burst in the farmer's field next door, and scatter all the cows. I think I told you

yesterday about our neighbours, a French farmer
and his wife, an old grannie, and four little girls,
and how amused they were by the sound of the
shells. Well, the next one hit the roof of their
farm, and sent most of it up in a cloud of red smoke
and brick dust. Then I remember running up the
road, with the doctor's pyjamas twinkling in front
of me, shouting to the people to come out. The
man came out, and three of the little girls, wounded
and crying, and after them, the poor old woman,
who was also badly hurt. We guided them along
the road as best we could, back to our own farm,
but the shells were still coming, and several times
we had to take shelter in the ditch. Then I came
off to rouse my own platoon, and get them down
into the cellars, and while I was away, the Germans
scored four direct hits on our own farm, and brought
most of the wall on my bed; I can't make out
why Clark, who was in the room at the time, escaped
without a scratch. In twenty minutes it was all
over; we had seen nothing of Sophie and her
mother, and were very much afraid they had
been killed; but that plucky girl had stayed beside
her mother, who is an invalid, dressed her, and
guided her down to the cellar, where they were
both safe. Clemence, Amelie, and Simone had
their wounds dressed, and were taken off in our
ambulance; they will all recover in a few days

I think, but the old lady is more serious. It does
seem so cruel that those little girls, who were so
bright and jolly, and favourites with all the regiment,
should have to suffer for this war too; but, of
course, I think they should never have been allowed
to stay so near the firing line. Even now Sophie
and her father are determined to stay here beside
their cows, although they seem to have friends a
few miles away. . . . It took some time to clear
up the wreckage in our room; luckily nothing
had been set on fire, and there was great cheering
when we discovered that a bottle of whisky which
had been swept on to the floor was still unbroken!
The doctor must have been very cold by the time
his work was done, in a cold north wind, with only
a thin pair of pyjamas. He is a first-rate man,
and very good to all the French people round
about, so that they all love him. His French is
even worse than mine, but still he rattles along, and
they enjoy his mistakes.

Reserve Farm   May 31, 1915.

After our disturbance the night before I slept
in the open, and we were not shelled again. It was
a fine clear night but cold, and in the early morning
a heavy bombardment began somewhere, which
we shall hear about presently. To-day I spent

some weary hours hanging about in a village street, in case I should be called a witness to the character of a man in my platoon, who was being tried by court-martial for sleeping at his post. But after all I was never called, and the sentence of the court has not yet been declared. It's a serious thing for a sentry to be found sleeping, and there is no excuse now, for everyone has plenty of time to sleep in the day. This afternoon I went down to the trenches, hearing that the 91st were immediately on our left, and found Sholto, who just joined them a week ago. He was looking enormous in his kilt, and very brown, but he seems to have enjoyed his three months in the 4th Battalion at Plymouth, and though I think he regrets the 91st has come from war to peace, he mayn't find it quite so peaceful after another night. By all accounts they have had a strenuous time in their last trenches, and lost nearly 700 men in April and May. It's odd that chance should have set them down next door to us, but I don't know whether they will stay there very long. Our cat was killed yesterday by one of the shells, or else died of shock soon after. Amelie, Clemence, and Simone are all in hospital, but in good spirits, so Sophie tells us. Sophie is now running the whole farm single-handed. How these French girls do work! Sometimes she gets Maurice to carry water; Maurice is a refugee from Belgium, a funny little boy of thirteen, with a serious old man's face, as if he had been forced to grow up by the war. . . .

Reserve Farm : June 2, 1915.

We have been relieved to-night, but B company remains behind in some farms near the firing line until an hour before dawn, so we are sitting in a loft, waiting for the light to come ; it is a very sultry night. I have enjoyed these last five days very much, in spite of the shelling on Sunday morning ; the doctor is a pleasant companion, and I always like talking to a clever doctor, for he sees and hears and knows a lot. There is a lot of distant firing in the south, and I think the French must be pressing hard again. Nothing has happened here, and I think it would do everyone good now to be moved ; we are just too comfortable, and both officers and men lose their energy when the weather is so fine, and the trenches are so quiet. I don't suppose I shall see much of Sholto, but since we are now attached to the 27th Division we may meet occasionally ; the 91st have moved, so that they are not alongside of us any more. I have finished ' Richard Feverel ' ; I didn't like it so much at the second reading, although I liked the ' Egoist ' more ; but perhaps this wasn't the time or the place for reading

N

it. And I reread Tolstoi's 'Sevastopol,' which gives you wonderful pictures of what the town was like during the siege, and a lot of what he says about the feelings of people who are fighting are as true now as when they were written. The three little girls who were wounded are all getting on well in hospital ; they won't be so keen to watch shells bursting when they come back. Roads are getting very dusty, and the ditches smell worse than ever. I think there will be a good many mosquitoes, and, of course, 'infinite torment of flies ' ; that's to be expected when there's a midden in the centre of every group of farm buildings. There are the usual rumours to-night : that the German fleet is sunk, that President Wilson is assassinated, that the Turks have given up, and that the Russians have won an enormous victory ; after all these lies are no worse than the printed ones. I wonder if the Zeppelins have dropped bombs on Woolwich arsenal ?

Billets · June 3, 1915.

I have done very little to-day except sleep, the result of being up all last night. A large parcel of socks has arrived by post, and I sent them off to the company store ; a packet of cigarettes has also arrived Did I tell you that Mrs. Haldane had sent me another letter of instructions ? and also a new kind of respirator in a little vanity bag ? so now I am well armed. I was glad to hear of your fine weather at Rhuveag, and of the port-manteau rod ; what a pity that Edward Campbell couldn't stay for a week or two. I heard from Uncle Charlie too, very nice of him to write ; he was, I think, casting longing eyes from the hill above Cathlaw towards Ben-a'oen ; but I think you said there was some chance of getting him for a week-end. He would like to find his favourite orchis on the roadside again, just beyond the big rocks. It's very nice of you to write so often, but you must have so many letters, and I haven't really. For it's not easy to write to a man when you haven't the faintest idea where he is, or what he is doing, and that is the case with most of my friends at present. . . .

Trenches : June 5, 1915

We are back again in the old trenches, which we used to hold at the end of March, when the weather first began to get fine. There is a great difference since then ; the grass has grown so long everywhere that we can hardly see the German parapet, and the trees hide a great deal of front too, now that they are in full leaf. German shells have knocked down two or three more of the trees just behind us, and

N 2

have battered down most of what was left of the two farms. But the orchard is still very pretty, and the scars made by the 'Minen werfer' are disappearing. These trenches are much deeper than the others I have been in, for somehow or other they never were flooded so badly, so they still hold the original line of last October, through the middle of a wheat field which was never harvested. Now the wheat has sown itself, and is growing up everywhere in tall bunches on the parapet ; in fact, it is in the ear already. Sonia, the cat, is now the happy mother of three kittens, very pretty little kittens too. Never having known any home except this trench, I suppose they would be most indignant if our line went forward and left them. In the meantime they and their mother and three servants live in one dug-out, when they are not sprawling in the sun. We only had two days in billets last time, and are likely to have less and less as time goes on, but it's no more hardship now to live in the trenches permanently ; there's more work there through the night, but less through the day. I had a bathe yesterday in the very muddy river about two miles from our billets , about twenty men went in too. The water was warm enough, but the mud at the sides was black and evil smelling ; so much so, that I walked into the town in the afternoon to wash off the sediment. I saw one or two small perch and some water lillies, white and yellow, in a pool just separated from the main stream. There used to be a naval launch in the river, for bringing ammunition to a naval armoured train, which trundled up and down behind us, and bothered the Germans, because they never knew where it would turn up next. But now I think it has gone away, and the sailors are probably enjoying an inland voyage through the canals of France. An old French farmer, to whom I spoke the other day, said that if last winter had been as wet as some winters we should never have been able to stay in our trenches at all. He said we should have had to build platforms four feet above the ground instead of digging down below it. He was, by the way, the father of Sophie, Amelie, and Clemence, the three little girls who were wounded. They are all recovering except the little one, who had two pieces of shell in her leg, and I think they carried in pieces of her stockings with them. But perhaps she will pull through in spite of it. They have been shelling us at intervals all day, but we are well covered, and can laugh at shrapnel ; in fact, though they fired over thirty shells this morning, they never got me out of my blankets. I heard a distant sound, but just turned over and went to sleep again. It becomes harder and harder to find anything to put in my letters ; 'sat in dry ditch' is the beginning and end of my soldiering at present.

Trenches : June 6, 1915.

All is quiet to-day on the front held by the 93rd, except that fierce engagements go on night and day between the three kittens, and also between Sonia, the proud mother, and a small black terrier pup, called Satan Macpherson, who belongs to the machine-gun officer. Satan has the best intentions in the world, and is only anxious to do his best for the new army by paying a friendly call; but as soon as he attempts to advance, he is met with high explosive, and driven from his position at the point of the bayonet. Fighting still continues.

General X. visited our trenches this morning. He must, I think, be an uncle of my friend, who always had more uncles than I should have believed possible of any man not closely related to the Patriarchs. The General is a tall, genial, old gentleman, known among his division as Father Christmas, very lively on his feet; he has two long rows of medals, and wears glasses, perhaps, as someone suggested of another much decorated general, to save himself from colour blindness when he looks down at his ribbons. Our own Brigadier came round with him. The General stopped at one point in my trench and took a cautious peep through a periscope. ' There seems to be a road out there,' he said. ' Yes,' said the Brigadier, ' there's a road leading out towards the German lines.' 'Indeed!' said the General, 'and what steps are taken to guard it?' 'Patrols are sent out along it every night, sir.' I said nothing, but I knew the road, and knew that it did not exist till last night, when I sent out two of my men to cut it through the standing corn. It's best to leave one general to answer another general's questions whenever possible. Here, of course, we talk of our generals as small boys do of their schoolmasters. They may be secretly respected or admired, but, to hear us talk, you would suppose they were all nervous, excitable old gentlemen, doddering with age, hopelessly incompetent, and utterly ignorant of what a trench looks like, and even of the way to fire a rifle. All of which is not perhaps strictly true, for this one had, at any rate, a sense of humour. In this company, all except the officers were just carrying on as usual, which meant that, except for the sentries, you could see nothing except boots sticking out from the dug-outs, and hear nothing except a confused sound of snoring from within. In the next company, however, a zealous company commander had routed all his men out, and made them stand to arms at the parapet. The General looked at them and remarked, 'I suppose these are all the men who would be asleep if I were not coming round?' And, strange as it may seem, there are some generals famous for their courage There

used to be one in the next brigade to us who is well
known through the army by his nickname ' Inky
Bill.' I believe he rode out on a white charger,
rather like the great Russian Skobeleff at the siege
of Plevna, and was never hit, though often well
within range. In October, too, when we were re-
tiring off the ridge in front, and things were critical,
he was reported to have made ready to charge the
Germans, with his Brigade-Major, a few cooks, and
officers' servants. I see Captain Wreford-Brown,
D.S O., Northumberland Fusiliers, is killed ; a very
nice man, who came up in the train with me from
Rouen to rail-head. Latterly, I think he had been
an instructor at Sandhurst, but his medals showed
that he had seen a great deal of service on the N.W.
frontier and elsewhere. Someone in the corner,
who had *not* seen a great deal of service, was bucking
about what he and his regiment had done, or were
going to do. Wreford-Brown stood it for a time,
and then, when there was a pause, he said quietly,
' Well, personally, if I get through this war alive
without feeling I have disgraced myself publicly, I
shall be jolly well pleased ' I have got your pug-
garees, which I shall keep in case we go on trek ; here
in the trench I don't think I am likely to use them
much ; and I have your ' Sixty American Opinions '
too. They are very encouraging, even if they are
selected from what Americans call ' highbrow ' class

of lawyers, authors, and college presidents. The names, of course, are Anglo-Saxon. I remember noticing that, in spite of the immense immigration from other countries, the names in the Roll of Congress for 1915 were mostly British. Base-ball players seemed to show a majority of Irishmen; clothing trades were in the hands of queer-sounding combinations, from the south-east of Europe I suspect, just like our Jews in the East End, who make so many soldiers' uniforms; while Greeks seem to corner the fruit trade. These professions which run with nationality are rather curious. We have the Italian and his organ, the Portuguese with his strings of onions, the Highland policeman, and the Clydeside engineer, who seems as indispensable as oil in every ship's engine-room. But in reading American and every other 'opinion,' I notice more and more what strength the invasion of Belgium gave to our case for going to war If the Germans had invaded France straight across her own frontiers, we should have been just as much bound in honour to support her against an unprovoked attack. But it would not have been nearly so clear to the rest of the world that it was the right thing for us to do. Germany supplied us and the rest of the world with a very striking illustration of what her methods would lead to, sooner or later, if any western country crossed her. Belgium is by far the weakest power in the field, but, in a way, she has been more trouble to Germany than the rest of us put together, and will be for years to come, which shows that brute force isn't the only thing which counts, even in modern war.

The bog-myrtle was still very sweet when it arrived. Did you ever read a poem with the verse in it ?

> From the lone shieling, and the misty island
> Mountains divide us, and a waste of seas,
> But still the blood is warm, the heart is Highland,
> And we in dreams behold the Hebrides.

There are very few real Highlanders in this regiment now, though I have one in my platoon from Strath Conon in Ross-shire.

Trenches : June 8, 1915.

We had a birthday party last night for Clark ; the dug-out was like an oven, and everybody was sweltering in their shirt sleeves and thinking of iced drinks ; but we had tinned asparagus and a boned fowl, and three bottles of very sticky sweet champagne, which had been unearthed somewhere in the town, the last of the cellar, I expect.

To-day was even hotter ; a thunder shower laid the dust for a bit, and brought out a pleasant smell of wet earth and wet grass—but it's still very close. The Brigadier came round again, but he or his staff had forgotten the politeness of princes, and they were nearly an hour late—perhaps they felt faint and had to sit down on the way. I like the heat when I am moving about, but I don't like sitting or lying still in it, and we shall have 'infinite torment of flies' before the summer is out.

Yet another respirator has been issued to me, a kind of helmet this time through which I can make my voice heard to give orders; the other gagged me most effectually. The following information is published in our official summary :

' It is stated by a refugee recently escaped from Lille, that, as the result of a fancy dress dance given there by the Germans on Christmas Eve, one of the local ladies who had participated in the festivities found the next morning that the words " Gott strafe England " had been tattooed on her person.' The champagne, I'm afraid, must have been very good if she never noticed she was being tattooed till the cold light of morning; or do you think the atmosphere was so charged with hate that the words printed themselves by some wireless process—just as Bloody Mary said they would find ' Calais ' written on her heart ?

How ridiculous the Germans have made themselves with their ' Gott strafe England ' ! Our newspapers have taken up a great many silly cries, but none quite so silly as that.

It will take a good deal more hammering to force the lock at the Dardanelles. I was glad Winston Churchill said so clearly at Dundee that it was vitally important to the course of the war in the main theatre—though perhaps it would have come a little more effectively from someone else's mouth. I have thought all along that if Russia is to carry on the war with her new armies she must get an outlet to the rest of the world. She has less factories than we, and she can buy neither raw material nor finished explosives, except in very small quantities carried across Siberia from Japan.

The general elections in Greece are due this month I wonder what our old friend Eleutherios Venizelos will do Daisy and I became familiar with his face on posters in Athens. He is *not* in the least like Pericles, although his fond admirers say he is, for a very ugly man with spectacles, a huge nose, a stubbly beard, and a tall hat cannot pose as an ancient Greek ; but he must be one of the ablest men in Europe, and if he had had his way I expect the Greeks would be marching through Macedonia to take the Turks in the flank

Trenches   June 9, 1915.

So you got an extension of leave, and Helen
had a Red Cross nurse to herself on her visit.   I
wonder whether the willow-herb was in flower just
below the cottage across the ford, and whether
the rhododendrons were as fine as last year ; not
quite, I expect, for we couldn't have two such good
years running.   Here we are just in the middle
of a thunder-storm, but the noise of thunder sounds
rather tame and ordinary compared with a shell ;
at least there's nothing frightening in it, and
no whistling pieces to follow.   I have finished
' Cranford,' which I never read before ; it doesn't
quicken the pulse, or even tickle the ribs, but
everything is drawn with such a delicate touch,
that it's a pleasure to read.   Now I have begun
another book of peace, though I believe it must
have been written in the middle of the twenty-five
years' struggle with Napoleon.   I mean ' Sense and
Sensibility.'   One thing I can never quite get over
in reading an old-fashioned book ; that is the
feeling that language, which would be affected
to-day, must always have been a little affected ;
yet I know it wasn't really.   ' Is there a felicity
in the world,' said Marianne, having ' ascended '
the downs ' superior ' to this ?   ' Margaret, let us
walk here at least two hours.'   If she was human

enough for the second sentence, the first must have been her natural way of speaking. I wish you would give me as a birthday present, Gibbon in Everyman's ; send out a couple of volumes at a time, then I can get rid of them as I read them. For even though it takes time and men and ships to force the Dardanelles, I think the story of Constantinople will be taken up again where it was left in 1455. It's curious to think of the two graveyards ; one beside the Bosphorus, where all the British soldiers were buried who died in Florence Nightingale's hospitals at Scutari, after fighting for the Turk against the Russian, and now this new one beside the Dardanelles, where we are fighting for the Russian against the Turk.

Trenches · June 10, 1915

I haven't had any letters for a day or two, but I hope Uncle Charlie has broken the spell over the loch. It's still very hot and close here ; neither aeroplanes nor artillery can observe much, so they have been quiet. There must have been a lot of exaggeration about the shortage of shells, by people who love to put their finger on one fault and explain everything by harping on that. I was asking an artillery officer yesterday about it ; he had been all through the recent fighting at Ypres.

He said there was never any question of a limit
there, except the difficulty in getting up supplies
from the parks to the guns quick enough, but they
could fire as many rounds as they pleased. Here,
of course, when nothing particular is going on, they
are strictly limited. Another battery, which was
here a few days ago, had been just behind the
Canadians when the gas was first used on April 22.
When the Germans passed their flank, they turned
their guns round, so that they were firing in
two absolutely opposite directions, with alternate
sections of two guns. They had been gassed too
later on, at least 2000 yards behind the firing
line. The guns were in a hollow, and suddenly
they saw the gas come rolling over the brow in
front like a cloud, but owing to their respirators
they didn't suffer much. The only officer badly
gassed was, curiously enough, Tom's old friend
Tinné, the rowing Blue (you know the famous
picture of the supper-party in his rooms in fancy
dress); and he was running round kicking out the
men, many of whom were asleep at the time.
When it was all over, they found their pet dog
dead, killed by the gas just where he lay curled up
asleep. We go back into billets to-night. I hear
the 91st will be out too, so I may see Sholto. . . .

Billets · June 12, 1915.

Your bog-myrtle came to-day, still very sweet, and a scent like that always stirs the memory more than any writing, or talking, or sketching can do. There's a passage in Homer which I'm very fond of, where he casts about for something to give the idea of swiftness, and instead of taking lightning or the flight of an arrow, he says, like the thought of a man who has travelled to many places, and sits at home thinking to himself, ' I wish I was there or there.' But I shouldn't be at all happy at Rhuveag just now, so I don't really want to be there, except to see you. I have just come in from a walk with the doctor, along a road which runs south parallel to the firing line, and a mile behind it. We should have been in La Bassee before evening if we had followed it along. The country was very pretty; tall hedges with wild roses in them, grass very long and green, and pollard willows standing beside the black ditches, which are now mostly covered with duckweed and water crowfoot. The willow is a prettier tree than the olive, I think; it has much the same grey-green colour when the leaves turn over, but the branches are more graceful. The farms were mostly deserted, and shell holes through the roof and walls showed the necessity; but of course there

are soldiers, gunners especially, billeted everywhere, and one or two stray inhabitants, who have
escaped so many times that now they feel they
can't be hit ; curious how a lot of narrow escapes
either break a man's nerve altogether, or give
him ten times the confidence that he had before.
There are no vineyards so far north as this, but
vines climbing all along the cottages and houses,
as they used to do in the villages round Winchester.
I saw one artilleryman busy building an observation post, just like a large bird's nest 60 feet up in
a poplar tree ; that is the great difficulty in this
flat enclosed country, to observe the fire of modern
long range guns. Little shops are springing up
everywhere, and there are notice boards in windows
to say that eggs and milk and ' chips ' are sold. . . .
We go back into trenches to-night, to a new bit of
trench ; that means dining early, so I must get
ready.

Trenches : June 13, 1915.

We were a very long time in getting into our
new trenches last night, for the guides had been
sent to the wrong place ; the night was very dark,
and we wandered about in a perfect rabbit warren
of trenches, where even the occupiers did not
seem to know the way. Luckily, the Germans
were unusually quiet, for if they had started shelling

o

us when we were blocked in the communication trenches, or had showered grenades over the parapet as they had done the night before, they might have made a large bag. This used to be the hottest corner in this part of the line, but it's only luke-warm now. My trench is only 70 yards from the German front trench, so we can only use loopholes and cannot put heads up by day. I think I described the place to you once before ; it's very like the lower deck of a ship, for the trench is roofed over, to give protection against rifle grenades, bombs, and trench mortar ' sausages,' which are freely offered at times, and in place of portholes, there are iron plates with sliding shutters, in case we have to fire. The parapet is very thick, but it could not have been built at all, if it had not been begun and finished in the days of peace which followed the New Year, when both sides were too wretched with mud and water to bother about firing. Then, when both had made themselves reasonably comfortable, they went at it again. There are a great many graves scattered about just behind the trench, for the Germans are really on three sides of us here, and it takes a long time to get in and out. But there is one advantage of being so near, that they can hardly shell us for fear of hitting their own men. We have to keep boots and equipment on day and night, for the trenches are too close together to make it possible to put up wire, and now, of course, there is always the chance of gas, though we are well provided against that. Perhaps all this sounds a great deal worse than it really is, for we have had a very quiet day, with very little firing, and I don't think it's any worse than our old lines used to be. I had one piece of luck, for the 91st have moved along a little to our left, and I found Sholto there this morning, very brown and big . . . I wish he had come to this battalion, and I think he misses some of his friends in the 4th. He has been in the trenches a fortnight without a break We have two bomb catapults, but I think the elastic is wearing out, as it does with all catapults. I wish I had something which would destroy Bombilius Major, who is holding this trench in great force, and seems to think the sand-bags are put there for him to bask on them. There is a kind of biting house-fly too. . . . There are no gardens here, there has always been too much to do, and much more than rain used to fall from the sky. . . .

Trenches : June 14, 1915

We had a lively afternoon yesterday, for a trench mortar battery came along to wake the

Germans up. They started with 33-pounder bombs, like a big turnip with a long handle, and we watched them sailing through the air, with the handle spinning round. But out of twenty large bombs, only eight went off. Then the Germans brought out their sausage machine, and started to reply. The sausage machine throws up a long bomb like a rolling-pin, which makes a most infernal noise. We could hear the report and see them come rocketing over a tall row of trees just above our trenches, tumbling over and over in the air. I felt like a small boy at Winchester waiting for high catches in the deep field, for the sausage seemed to hang in the air above your head, while, to use Daddy's favourite expression, your past life rose before you like a cloud, and you wondered when the thing was going to come down, and whether it would go right over, or hit a branch and drop straight on your head; and all the time it seemed to hang there, tumbling round and round. Luckily, they all went over the fire trench where I was standing, but one sausage was rude enough to come into our company trench quarters, where it wrecked Clark's house, and very nearly spoilt the dinner. It was really very funny to see them. We replied with two smaller mortars, which showered turnips on them until their sausage machine was damaged or silenced for want of sausages. But by that time they were thoroughly angry, and had sent word to their artillery, which put more than thirty shells over our heads, and into the trenches on our left. They also showered rifle-grenades on us, to which we replied in kind, and for a while there was quite a battle with turnips, sausages, rifle-grenades, and shells all flying through the air, and bursting round about. But, in spite of all this frightfulness, no one in this company was hit. For some time, however, we all had a sausage eye, and kept looking up anxiously when a swallow passed the trees, and in the evening when three or four large bats came out, I kept on seeing them past the corner of my spectacles, and looking round anxiously for cover. The artillery officer who runs the trench mortar battery was in my trench, and his orderly at the telephone laughed so much that he could hardly pass the orders; presently, however, a sausage broke all his wires behind, so he had to go out and mend them under fire. We have just begun the same evening sport again, but we have no more of the big bombs, and sausages are scarce too. . . .

Trenches : June 16, 1915.

It must have been a hot day if it tempted you to swim. . . . It's very hot again here, though the nights are still cool. Bombilius is a greater plague than ever. I almost wish we could have a gas attack in order to get rid of him. They tell me that where the gas has passed out at Ypres there is not a fly to be seen anywhere, so it has some compensations. We have been getting cherries from an orchard just behind the trenches of the 91st, and strawberries can be had when we are in billets, but at present we only come out for two days at a time. Gordon, our brigadier, has left us to take up command of a division at home, and the Colonel of the Cameronians succeeds him. . . . Some of the men are getting leave again, but there will be none for officers, except on doctor's orders. If we did more fighting in this part of the world, we should get more leave, but we can't have it both ways. . . . We seem to be on the move again at both ends of our line.

Trenches : Waterloo Day, June 18, 1915.

I got such a packet of letters last night that I spent the time when I should have been writing to you in reading them. The Invernenty burn must be just the same as ever, and I should like to hear it and the whaups, if they are still whistling in June. I hope the cuckoo has not disappointed Francis of his war-baby. Pipits, and other small birds who are favoured with these blessings, seem to give them far more attention than they would give their own respectable families, and some of the letter writers in the papers are inclined to do the same. Some sparrows have built a straw nest in a tree just above my trench, and the young birds should be very precocious, for they must have a strenuous life. At that height they needn't fear very much except shrapnel, but the tree itself is bleeding to death, for its trunk near the ground has been riddled through and through with bullets. I quite expected that the Germans would remind us of Waterloo—*La Belle Alliance*, as they call it—for they are quite as convinced that Blücher did everything as we are that it was Wellington's battle. Sure enough, when I was sitting quietly in my dug-out at 3.30. A.M., I heard a sudden noise, and our old friends the sausages began to hurtle through the air. They wrecked one bit of our trench pretty thoroughly, but the only one which came near me, bounced on the parapet and, after hesitating a little, decided to stay outside. The early morning sun was in our eyes, so that it was difficult to ' mark over,' and the noise was soon too loud to hear them coming. For a howitzer battery opened on our reserve trench fifty yards behind, and did some very pretty shooting, and two or three field batteries began firing shrapnel. So we had a lively half-hour, and were surprised to find when it was all over that our losses were only one man killed and three wounded ; we were very lucky to get off so lightly. The sausage was just the same as before. ' It puts yer in mind of a polony,' as one of my men said to me. One of them fell in a ditch, where it sent up a fountain of most evil-smelling mud, and some buried German ammunition. All the day before we had peace, and all to-day too since early morning, though our heavy howitzers have been busy on some target a long way behind their front line. We are relieved to-night, and go back into billets for two days. There was a very funny scene to-day, when a prisoner for court-martial, not of this regiment, objected to being tried by a major in the Middlesex, because he said the major was ' too much of a religious cove.' The objection was allowed ; whether based on truth or not, I can't say, but a suitable Gallio was found to preside over the court. I went along and saw Sholto this evening, and showed him some photos of his nieces which reached me last night, together with a budget of letters from Glenairley. I'll send them home presently, but I like to have them here in the trenches and look at them. The ' mink ' has been busy with Al's hens again, but his old ' factor ' Harry Q. is still with him. Marion C. will be glad to know that. . . . I think that it was a wise man who said that every country gets the Jews which it deserves, and ours have done well for us on the whole. After Dizzy, it's too late to start Jew-baiting, though if Dizzy hadn't been so full of visions in the Near East, and faith in the Oriental Turk, we might not have backed the wrong horse in 1878, and might have saved our troubles in the Dardanelles to-day. This letter should reach you on my birthday, or thereabouts. At Cargilfield I used to have great luck in spending my birthday at home, but that won't happen this year. However, I think I shall have a very happy birthday out here, and you must let it be a cheerful day at home. Of course, I wish that I could see a chance of getting back to my work, for twenty-six seems rather late to be starting my way in the world. Perhaps a year out here would make me a better man, if not a better barrister; sometimes I think I am learning a lot, sometimes it all seems sheer waste. But, anyway, until we win this war, I really care very little what happens to me or to anyone else, though, naturally, I want to come back, and want my friends to come back too.

Billets : June 20, 1915.

We go back to the trenches again to-night, to our old line, which, as a rule, is not so lively. But the German guns have been rather active these last few days. Personally, I think they are making a noise to cover the withdrawal of most of their infantry. I'm sure there are very few men in the trenches in front of us, and that most of them have gone north or south to the more critical points. But, of course, they leave wire and machine-guns behind them, so that we can't stroll across. Yesterday morning they put 105 shells into a space no longer than the path from Rhuveag door to the gate (about 80 yards) ; marvellous shooting ! too good in fact, for they never got the battery which they were firing at ; but if these shells had scattered, they would certainly have knocked our guns out. To-day they shelled our billets, wounding three men, one from my platoon.

I marched a party of men for a bath in a factory yesterday, a factory for bleaching linen, with great wooden vats full of hot water, and some of cold, so that you could take a plunge afterwards. I was so pleased with the chance of a wash that I jumped in without taking off my wrist watch, but it does not seem to have suffered. . . . I saw Sholto again yesterday; he had a very comfortable billet ; a pale blue carpet, art paper on the walls, and a spring mattress, so that at 5.30 P.M. I could hardly wake him up. But he has had a long spell in the trenches. From what he tells me, I seem to have outlasted all but a very few of the 4th Battalion who came out with or before me ; one killed, but several wounded, and others sick. I don't hear of much typhoid, or dangerous disease, but there is a lot of flu, or low fever, which gives men a temperature for a day or two, and leaves them rather ' piano.' I had hoped he would be able to dine with me. Unfortunately, he had to go digging, so I had to have my dinner alone—in the house where we get our hot baths. The housekeeper will give you a very nice dinner there, very nicely served and marvellously cheap. So I enjoyed a clean cloth, and clean glass and silver, new peas, potatoes, strawberries, and cherries—in fact all the delights of the season. . . . How splendidly the French are fighting ! I do admire the way they are facing this war. They seem to have made a calm resolution to drive the Germans out of their country, no matter what the cost, and they will do it. I see that in the Crimean War, they and we only lost some 10,000 killed between us. Yet I always thought of that as a big enough war. . . .

Trenches : June 21, 1915.

We are back again in a peaceful trench, 500 yards from the Germans, and until they shell us we can sit at ease, enjoying the sunshine, and the wind in the corn. It has been a very hot day, until this breeze sprang up, and I spent most of the morning waiting in a dusty street, while an interminable court-martial dragged itself along. One of my men had been found sleeping on sentry, and he called me as a witness that he had complained some time ago of trouble with his eyes, though why he should make that an excuse for shutting his ears too, I don't understand, and I don't think the court will either. I was annoyed at wasting a morning over evidence which only took a minute, more especially because last night, to my great surprise and delight, I found A. G. Heath,[1] of New College, now of the West Kents, was attached to us for instruction. He has just come out with another division of K.'s army. It was very pleasant to see him again, and to get news of a great many friends. But he will go off again to-night, and we are not very likely to meet again. I think the new army are very well trained, very fit, and very keen ; in fact, I believe they would astonish Europe if we could only get the Germans

[1] Fellow of New College, Oxford : he was killed in action in France on October 8, 1915.

on the move again. They seem to march miles every day without tiring, while we have hardly marched more than three miles in the last three months. This letter never was finished yesterday, for there was a lot to do ; two platoons of West Kents came down to us, and we had to get them in quickly before a patrol went out to try and get a prisoner. They got no prisoner, but secured a helmet and a greatcoat which some German threw away. So they found out what regiment was opposite, which was what they really wanted to do. To-day I can just imagine what a tired hostess feels like at the end of a strenuous day, for I have been trotting round answering questions, and trying to pretend that life in the trenches is desperately interesting, which it isn't, when you would very much like to be asleep if your guests were not there to be entertained. However, Heath has stayed till this evening. . . . The French guns are still thundering away in the far distance night and day ; they seem to have any quantity of shells, and I bet the Germans opposite them are wishing they had never come to France, for I think the French are driving them out of each new position before they have had time to dig themselves in properly, which must be most exhausting work, when they are always digging against time, and always just too late. . . .

Trenches : June 23, 1915.

My birthday, like almost every other day, has been quiet enough, though this last half-hour our guns have been trying to knock out a German machine-gun which we had spotted opposite us, and the Germans have been replying with shrapnel on our trenches. It amuses the West Kents who have come in to be instructed, and are quite disappointed if there is nothing doing. We have been hosts again to two more officers, one a Balliol man, whom I afterwards discovered to have been at Loretto. He had known Ronald and Sholto ; said that Ronald not only made a tremendous impression in the year that he was head, but left a tradition after him for years, and that there was a school of followers who held him up as a pattern of the Loretto spirit. We had quite a little fight the other night. Bankier took out a strong patrol in front here, to see if he could get a German trench ; he couldn't manage that, but, on the left, one of our patrol came into touch with the Germans in the long grass. First of all, they cut off a small party under a sergeant, one of our genuine Highlanders from Loch Awe side ; he charged them, yelling, with a revolver in each hand, and laid out seven of them. Then he came back with another party, and recovered two of his men who were badly wounded—driving the Germans off, who retired past another party of ours who were lying further out in the grass. They also dropped some Germans, and captured a helmet and a greatcoat which were thrown away in the rush; so that we know now that we have the 179th Saxon regiment opposite us, and G H.Q. were very much pleased with this information. We lost one man missing; but I think the Germans were scared, for they have been playing their search-lights on our front, and have brought up new machine-guns. The French are still thundering away to the south, good luck to them. They have done splendidly, and the Germans opposite them must wish they had never been born. I don't expect to see any great capture or surrender, but I think the angle which Soissons makes in our line may be driven in. . . . They are still shelling us, but one must just sit tight, and believe in one's luck; no one has been hit yet.

Trenches: June 24, 1915.

We have had another peaceful day instructing the West Kents. . . . We have just had a heavy thunder-storm, and everything is still dripping, as you will see from this paper. A very little rain makes the surface as slippery as ever, but it dries quickly now. The wheat which has sown itself in the fields round about will soon be ripening, and we are threatened with a plague of mice. I saw ever so many while I was on watch early this morning, playing about among the sand-bags ; they will soon eat holes in them, but a sand-bag full of wet earth has a short life in any case. After a couple of months they get too rotten to lift. I don't remember the loch which you describe as being beyond Ben Chion ; does it run out into Glengyle, or into the head of the Lochlarig stream ? The bathing must have been splendid. I had a letter from Laura last night, most enthusiastic about Rhuveag, but I was surprised to hear that she had never been there before. We are not likely to have guests in these other trenches, and I will try to write a longer letter to-morrow.

Trenches : June 25, 1915.

I find Sholto next door to me again, so this afternoon he came across for tea, and we made a beginning on the birthday cake, which is a wonderful creation, decorated with the flags of the Allies as well as my initials. It did not arrive till last night, possibly because it was dated for the 25th ; but it's a very good cake inside as well as out. Our bomb officer got a small china war baby from it ; he learnt earlier in the day that he had got the Military Cross, so that it was an eventful day for him. Another subaltern has also got the Military Cross for good work in the trenches, and since he was in charge of the successful patrol the other night he has been recommended for something more. I hear that Bankier is recommended too. We have been very peaceful here to-day ; the Germans are 350 yards away on our right, and nearly 1000 yards straight in front, with a wide field of blood-red poppies in between. There is a picturesque village, or what remains of one, on the far side, and beyond its whitewashed walls and ruined gables, the wooded ridge, behind which are the German batteries. It has been rather a gloomy day of rain and thunder ; rain much needed for the crops, if there had been any just here. I like the poem which you copied from the *Spectator*, but I

P

still think the front is very much less terrible than the 'back'; of course, I have seen no desperate fighting, but here in the trenches the wounded are dressed and taken away so quickly, and, as a rule, they suffer very little until their wounds get stiff; and when men are killed we do not see their homes. There are moments of suspense—for instance, last night when we were moving along an open road just behind the trenches, two shells suddenly swooped down out of the darkness, and burst not far behind my platoon. The men stepped out briskly, but there were no more, although I quite expected them, and was glad when we were all under cover again. I take no risks, except, perhaps, sometimes the risk of being thought afraid, for I am convinced that the officer who gets killed when he needn't be is doing no service to himself or to his men; and I have heard of so many being killed when there was no need. If only I had as many brothers at home as Sholto, I should be very happy. After all, to be killed fighting for a cause like ours is the greatest honour a man can win, and that is how we should try to look at it, as something far greater than a V.C. or any other honour to the living. Your letter describing the sunset over Ben Chion came last night. How well I can imagine it! We often have beautiful sunset skies here; but I think you miss something in a sunset unless there are reflections in still water, or unless the sun sets over the sea. We go back into billets on Sunday, I think, if the present arrangement holds good.

Trenches . June 26, 1915

The rain yesterday brought back memories of February, and I went to sleep once more with each foot thrust into an empty sand-bag, to keep some of the mud from my blanket. But to-day all is dry again with a sunny south wind. The field of poppies in front is really a marvellous sight ; they look to me crimson rather than scarlet, and the colour is set of by some very white sand-bags and lining on the German parapet behind. The country on the wooded ridge which the Germans hold looks very English, so much so that the gunners say they can see the vicar's daughter going along to play tennis every afternoon. There really is a female figure, dressed in white, who moves along a road at about the same time every day. . .

Thank you very much for Gibbon ; he was a marvellous man, to carry such a weight of learning with so much ease, and though research has completely changed the study of classics in the last fifty years, he still stands alone.

P 2

Trenches : June 27, 1915.

The 91st are moving along to relieve us to-night. It's just starting to rain very heavily, so we are lucky to be moving out. Nothing has happened ; some men were wounded by rifle grenades this morning, but not in this company. The Germans have changed their tactics very much since I came out ; they used to snipe ceaselessly all day and all night. Now they remain quiet as a rule, unless we stir them up. It would be better, I think, to be rather more active, for it seems to me that in this trench warfare both sides made the mistake of thinking that the most important thing to do was to strengthen their own position, whereas it was really more important to prevent the other side from doing so. In the wet weather it was natural that officers and men should think first how they could make an island of refuge in the seas of mud, and then strengthen their parapets to keep out bullets, and run up wire on stakes. But it came to this, that we could not fire when we heard their parties working, because our own were out in front ; and now, having definitely passed from the defensive to the attack, we suffer from the strength of their positions, and are often hampered by our own wire. The same thing would probably happen if we were set down facing one another again ; but that's where a staff can help, just because they are warm and dry and comfortable, and can look ahead. Their judgment isn't inevitably biassed, as it is for the man on the spot, who is lying unprotected in a wet hole in the open, and only wants to be let alone. The same problem is always coming up ; our infantry don't want our guns to shell the trenches opposite, because they are sure to retaliate on us, but if they think they can do the most damage, our gunners ought to damn the infantry and shell away. It's worth losing guns too, if by lingering behind they can make great havoc before they are captured ; but that must be one of the most difficult parts of a general's work, to balance these losses and gains, and a man like Napoleon, with little human feeling, has an advantage. So have the Germans at times, being more careless of human life. Whatever may be right in peace, I'm sure Radical politics are the only politics for war ; never to be content with things as they are. If you don't make the enemy do something, he'll make you do it, and force his time and place upon you. I don't know in the least whether we are preparing a great series of attacks, or whether we are concentrating our efforts on the Dardanelles. We must get through there before the autumn, if we want the Russians to help us effectively next winter. I don't see the slightest prospect of peace before next summer, but I see less prospect than ever that the Germans will be able to make a peace favourable to themselves. . . . You will have heard that Ronald Campbell was shot through the jaw a week ago ; a stray bullet while he was digging trenches behind the line. His luck is out in this war—or else he is lucky, if one looks at it the other way, for hospital with a severe wound is the safest place for any man at present. . . .

Billets : June 28, 1915

We had a long roundabout march back from our trenches last night, but were in billets before midnight. I always like walking on a summer night, and there's a peculiar pleasure in it when you are leaving the trenches. The rain had cleared off, and the moon was full. We fell in quietly on a road just behind the trench, as soon as the sentries had been relieved, and moved off by a track through the deserted fields. The first few hundred yards are always a little anxious, for there is a chance that a star-shell or search-light will discover you, or that the clink of rifles or shuffle of feet will be heard. But all went well, and we soon lost sight of the braziers and line of twinkling lights, which is all you see of the breastworks from behind at night. It was very still and quiet, with a smell of summer in the air, a change from the trenches, which often smell of chloride of lime, if they do not

smell of something worse, and the crack of the
rifles sounded fainter and fainter behind us, while,
at long intervals, a bullet would come lisping past.
Presently we reached a road, still showing white,
in spite of the weeds invading it from either side,
and followed it for a mile or more, parallel to the
firing line, with star-shells lighting up the level
ground and rows of poppies in the distance. The
farms are mostly ruined, though a light on the
sheltered side still shows when a telephone or headquarters' guard is there; and you can see the
sky through the battered roof, and the black holes
where the shells have gone through the thin brick
walls without bursting. I saw a German gun put
four through one gable-end one day, four successive
shots—good shooting ! I heard Sholto's voice in
the dark, as he led his platoon along, but did
not see him again. When I got back into billets,
I found a letter from Ralph Fowler waiting for me,
written of course before he was wounded. He spoke
of the difficulty of getting water, and of protecting
their line among broken sand-hills from enfilading,
but he said that from the head of some of the
ravines, they had beautiful views of Imbros and the
other islands. I heard from Stainton too to-day—
better, but on leave till September 1, and very
impatient to be back.

Billets : June 30, 1915.

What am I to say to you that I have not said fifty times before ? There is no change in the British front ; there have been showers, but it is clearing up again, and will soon be as hot as ever. For once I did see a new place to-day by walking a mile further along a road than I had been before ; there was not much to see—a deserted village with a wide street, almost empty, except for a few artillery men, and a ruined church, the doors of which were barricaded, I suppose to keep out spies or careless soldiers who might draw fire on the village again by climbing up the tower. The church seemed to have a foundation of old stone, but was finished off in brick. I wonder if for the same reason as Eton College buildings, which Henry VI began in stone before the Wars of the Roses, and which were finished above in brick, because after the wars stone was too expensive. There was a rank and hideous cemetery round about it, clumsy iron crosses instead of tombstones, and no old monuments at all. I wonder whether they were swept away in the Revolution with so much of old France. But I notice that even in this republican country you have ' Monsieur ' inscribed on your cross, if you can afford a better one than your neighbours. The country was flat and placidly pretty, red-tiled farms, cows, orchards, wheat fields. We asked one old man whether any of his cows had been killed, but he said no, but pointed to a big shell hole, and said in tones of infinite scorn, 'Les Anglais ont fouillé dedans'; so they had, 'mais les Français fouillent aussi,' and come running out with picks and spades as soon as a shell has fallen. I believe they get good prices for the fuses and other souvenirs in Paris. We called on our way back to make some inquiries about a supposed spy; lights had been reported on the nights when the battalions in this brigade relieved one another, but I don't think there is anything in it.

I was walking with a man who speaks French perfectly, Captain Irvine of this regiment; he was A.D.C. in Mauritius before war broke out and had to speak to the French sugar planters there, and he has since married a French girl. I have been inoculated for typhoid again, and the muscle of my arm is a bit stiff to-day, but otherwise it has not affected me. There is amazingly little typhoid or enteric among the British troops, but I hear the French have a great many cases, and that the Germans are even worse! I enclose a letter from Harold Edgell, who, like all educated Americans, seems very far from 'neutral.' I saw a good deal of him and his wife in the first fortnight after war was declared. The Champollion whom he speaks of was a grandson of the Professor Champollion who, I think, first deciphered the Rosetta stone, and so found the key to all the hieroglyphics in Egypt.

Billets : July 1, 1915.

It's a grey day, inclined to rain ; this northern corner of France is very like England, and seems to have almost exactly the same weather, perhaps a little hotter when the winds come to it across Europe instead of across the Channel. I had been enjoying a different billet, with a bed, and actually *sheets*, the first I have slept in since I left England, and except for one night in London, the first since I last left home. But early this morning I got up, wakened by our batteries which suddenly became noisy, and when I was satisfied that they weren't going to shell us back, and was returning to bed, behold ! insects of a size and splendour which I had hardly imagined. Perhaps they are fond of exercise in the early morning ; anyway I was glad that it was my last night, and not my first, or I might not have slept so sound ; their attack was beaten off with heavy loss, for they were too fat to run, and I have plenty of Keating's powder left.

Another parcel of dried fruit has arrived, but as we had not finished the last, I think I shall give it to my platoon. The *Sphere* never comes now.

I don't mind for myself, because I always see it
in the mess, but if you are ordering it, it ought to
come, and the men might like to see it. Send me
on two copies of Forbes-Mitchell's ' Reminiscences
of the Indian Mutiny,' Macmillan's 1s. series;
he was a sergeant in the 93rd, and I remember
that at Sunderland two copies which I gave my
platoon were very popular.

There is really *nothing* to make a letter.

Trenches: July 2, 1915.

I was very sorry indeed to hear last night from
Sholto that Eric Colbourne[1] had died of his wounds;
from what he told me before, I thought that there
was nothing serious; perhaps he was wounded
again later. It's very hard on Florence; seems
harder in a way because he gave up his work and
travelled so far to join, when no one would have
blamed him if he had stayed behind in Victoria.

The news from the Dardanelles this morning
seemed rather better, but if we are going to force
the Straits, I think we shall have to do it ourselves,
and not wait for Roumania or Bulgaria or Greece
or anybody else. They will fly to assist the con-
queror, as the French minister remarked, but I

---

[1] 2nd Lieut. Eric Colbourne, 1st Royal Berkshire Regiment
was mortally wounded at Cuinchy, 27th June, 1915—he had
been awarded the Military Cross for conspicuous bravery some
days before his death.

doubt very much whether they will move until it's all over with the Turk, bar the shouting.

I don't know that there's any weakening yet in the spirit of Germany, but I think there is a sharp difference of opinion between the Germans who want to annex Belgium now, and anything else they can lay hands on, and the Germans who don't want to annex anything, but are fighting because they were persuaded that they were going to be attacked. When the peace comes, these may realise that they weren't in danger of attack at all, but were rushed into war by the other party, and then will come the real change in German opinion and policy, if it comes at all.

We have had a few shells and a good many aeroplanes overhead this evening; otherwise we are as quiet as ever, and the rain has encouraged our gardens, which were getting very dry; we have some very pretty white lilies which I never expected to survive, being transplanted late in the spring.

I heard from Mitchison last night; he was out just in time for the last gas attack, but is now in billets somewhere behind Ypres, where only the very largest kind of shell can reach him. Bankier has come back with two bulldog puppies, which fight all day, though they can hardly carry the weight of their own heads yet. We have at least six dogs or puppies in this company alone now, a stray kitten or two, and a couple of leverets who live in a dug-out in the trench; but I wish we had some creature to feed on blue-bottles.

They have started giving leave again, but only one officer at a time, so that my turn will not come till September at the earliest, and very likely it will be stopped again if there is heavy fighting.

Trenches . July 4, 1915

We have had a sweltering hot day, as I know, for I was using a pick through the hottest part of the afternoon. But I feel ever so much better after digging hard for these last two days, and shall go on with it. After a period of inaction, the brigade staff have several new orders, which always means more digging for us; but it's good for the men to have more to do, for, as you say, keeping the hands busy gives the mind a rest too. There was a beautiful half-moon early this morning, with a bright morning star beside it. Last night was very warm and quiet, except for a strange display of rockets to the south of us—all colours, with showers of stars, green, blue, and red. We could not imagine what was happening, but it was only the artillery testing some new signals for directing fire in the dark. We have a wonderful trench of Madonna lilies in the garden. I don't know what it is that makes them glow in the half-light of morning or evening, but they are at their best then, and shining as I write.

If you should decide to go up to London, I should be quite glad to know how things are going on at the flat—in fact, before the winter, I should like you to rescue one or two belongings, particularly my photograph book, which has all the pictures of my travels in it, and several of Tom which you have not got anywhere else. It is more likely to be thumbed, too, than other books. There is no hurry about this, but clothes and everything else would be better at home, and they would leave more room for Belgium to spread herself. The hay fever is better now, more because the season is passing than by reason of the doctor's ' dopes,' I think ; it was rather troublesome in June, because it used to come on in the early morning, which is just the time of day when you hope to sleep. Now the only difficulty is with the flies, which swarm everywhere, and wake up and crawl upon you as soon as the sun gets strong in the morning ; please send me some fly-papers, the little ones which unroll are the best, and I should like a wrist strap for my left wrist, which is always apt to give when I do much shovelling. . . . And if you will give it to me for a birthday present, I should like to read a book which has just come out, ' Ordeal by

Battle,' by F. S. Oliver; he used to write a good deal for the *Round Table*, which, by the way, I have not seen lately; send me the current number and others as they come out . . . I used to take it regularly, but I'm afraid I have missed several quarters since last August. . . . To-day, in the middle of the peaceful sunny afternoon, a big shell suddenly swooped down from nowhere into the trench, killed five and wounded four. I remember Tom wrote from the Aisne that fifteen of his men had been put out of action by one of those Jack Johnsons. There is luck and bad luck with them; as a rule, they do surprisingly little damage. . . .

Trenches · July 5, 1915.

I started the day's work at 4 A.M by watering the garden, a long and muddy business, for I had to jump half the way down our wall to fill the watering-can, and stand on a slippery cask. The well is only a hole about six feet deep, which has been a trap to frogs and toads, until it swarms with them, but since all kinds of flies and moths and beetles tumble into it too, I expect they find a living. We have mignonette and corn-flowers coming on well now, with a lot of nasturtiums and canariensis to follow. The artillery have just finished their usual ' evening hate,' but we have only had small shells on our trenches, and no damage. We have a range-finding instrument now, which makes a very good telescope, and my men enjoy it, for one observes while the other snipes, so that you hear this sort of conversation: 'His heid coming up agen noo.' 'Ay, I seen it—he's taen his bonnet aff—he's bauldy-heided—I can see his broo.' Then they fire, and if it's a miss, the German often waves his cap in the air, before he goes down; but they are getting more cautious, for some have stayed up too long. But these are Saxons, with some sport in them. As a sample of the Bavarian, this letter was printed to-day, from a soldier in the Bavarian Guard Regiment. It was never posted, so I suppose it was found on his body. 'You will thus have a charming souvenir of a German warrior who has been right through the war from the very beginning, and has shot and bayoneted many Frenchmen, and also bayoneted many women. Dear Grete Maier, in five minutes, I bayoneted seven women and four young girls in the fighting at Batovile; my captain told me to shoot them, but I bayoneted the rabble of swine instead.' That's the sort of man whom I yet hope to see on the end of our bayonets. No one would suppose that our heavy howitzers were short of ammunition, for they seem to fire a good deal more than the Germans'; not all day of course, but every hour there are some shells going over. I suppose we have not enormous reserves, but we seem to have plenty for all ordinary needs. I think the Germans would like to settle the war on land on the best terms they could get, and then build an enormous fleet of submarines to blockade us at sea. They will try that when peace comes, I'm certain, if they still have a kick left in them; but I suppose we can do the same, and prevent their submarines from leaving harbour. . . .

Billets: July 7, 1915.

We spent last night in the farm where we were shelled six weeks ago, not very luxurious quarters, for there were only the bare boards to lie upon, and the mosquitoes, who had come swarming in at the shell holes, took advantage of my kilt. However, we only stayed there until daybreak; it was a very dark thundery evening, with puffs of hot wind, and when we had just left the trenches there was a terrific flash of lightning, which seemed to strike the ground just at our feet. I think we all expected to go flying into the air in little bits, for, at the moment, it seemed like a mine exploding or a gigantic shell. However it was the only flash, as these very big ones so often are, and we got under cover before most of the rain.

Q

I believe they shelled the farm again this morning, soon after we left it, and this afternoon they put some near our billets ; but the only one which came really near was a ' dead ' and did not explode. It's a nuisance being shelled in billets, for I was just going to sleep when I heard the first whistle, and after that you lie uncomfortably awake, listening for the next one and wondering whether it's any good going out to some other place. In the trenches you have got to stay there and look after your platoon, so there is an end of it, and it makes it much easier, but here in billets you always have the feeling that some other place might be safer. I sleep now in a house where a paralytic priest occupies the lower room, and we have to pass in and out with much grave and ceremonious saluting ; we must often disturb him, and I think he's ' wearying to get awa',' as Trotter says, for he sits there with his crucifix, and just lifts it up and down now and then. He has a fat priest friend who comes to give him consolation, the same priest whom I met riding his bicycle with the dress-guard to keep his skirts out of the wheel. But the friend seems to spend all his time talking to the women who own the house, and who are shrill voiced and rather impatient, I think, that their guest, like Charles II, ' takes such an unconscionable time in dying.'

People talk as if all France outside Brittany were anti-clerical, but this part of the country seems intensely Catholic, like the Belgians. Or rather the country people are Catholic, and I think in the big towns like Lille there is a bitter radical free-thinking opposition; these religious differences get mixed up with their labour troubles, and I think they had furious strikes in all the factories near here a little while ago before the war, with Jaures, the French novelist, who was assassinated at the beginning of the war, for their leader. By all the signs, we shall have strikes in the ten years following this war at home, which will make the coal strike and the railway strike seem small.

Billets : July 9, 1915.

I did not manage to write yesterday, for there were other things to think about. I started off to walk into the town with Bankier; just as we were leaving billets we heard a shell come over behind us, and both said we were glad to be going the other way. We had our bath and a stroll in the garden, which was peaceful and full of the later roses. Then, as we walked back, one of the men stopped us and said that some officers had been hit; only three shells had dropped near our billets, but they were unlucky ones, for the first killed six men and wounded five, and the third burst close beside Kennedy, Clark, and Irvine, who had gone across to inquire about the damage. Poor Irvine was killed outright. I was very sorry, for I liked him; he was full of interest in everything, and had married a French girl last winter to whom he was very much devoted. He spoke French so well that the old woman in his billet used to call him 'l'espion.' Kennedy was severely wounded in the arm; a great loss to the regiment, for he was a most capable adjutant, and an extremely nice man; and Clark was wounded in several places, not dangerously, I hope, though I doubt whether we shall see him out here for a long time to come. We shall miss him very much; he was quite untiring in his work for the company and extraordinarily brave; in fact, I can't imagine anyone could be cooler under fire. I did not see him, but Bankier rode down to the ambulance this morning before he was taken away and reported that he was still very cheerful. If his wounds heal well I shall be almost glad that he has gone, for he would have worn himself out by want of sleep, and would most certainly have been killed in any advance. But it is very hard lines for him, after coming through the whole campaign, and the company are very sad to lose him. Three captains by one shell! We shall have to get some more officers out from home.

Did you read Sir Ian Hamilton's long dispatch from the Dardanelles yesterday? It was extraordinarily well written, as one would expect from him, and gave me a very strong impression of the enormous odds against which they have been fighting out there; but more than all it gave me an impression of Sir Ian Hamilton's own ability; he seemed to have gripped the whole situation at once, to have realised the great difficulties, but to have conquered them, and if only he can get through, as I now think he will, the whole campaign will be one of the most marvellous feats of arms in history. Just think what it must mean to arrange for landing troops at half a dozen different points miles apart, when he could know nothing of the resistance to be met, except that it would be as strong as skill and the stubborn Turk could make it.

The Russian news is better too, but I expect that there will be another great German effort on this western front in August and September. . . .

Billets : July 11, 1915.

Daisy would tell you that we have lost our company commander, and we are not likely to get a nicer fellow, or a braver man. I hope his wounds wil not give trouble, but we shall not hear for some days now. Captains are scarce these days, and I don't know whether they will be able to spare any from the 3rd or 4th Battalion. There is a horrible lot of luck about these shells; if you can hear them coming and lie down, you aren't likely to get hit, even if they burst quite near you. To-day we have had no shells at all, though our guns made a great noise at 4 A.M., and I see a German observation balloon hanging in the distance; we also have one up a couple of miles back, a great sack drooping at one end. They are much steadier than aeroplanes for using telescopes, and there is no steering and balancing to be done; but, of course, they can't move, and are helpless in a wind. I always wonder that aeroplanes don't drop bombs on them, but I suppose they have air-craft guns sitting waiting underneath.

I have had quite a long walk to-day, seven miles at least, with the doctor. We went to visit his Christmas quarters, where he had had several civilian patients; but most of them had been shelled out of their houses since then, and had left for other parts of France. There were a great many roofs and walls in ruin, but a good many of the French people are still living there, sitting at their doorsteps and chatting with the soldiers in broken French and English. The churches had suffered most, and one brave old curé had been killed when

he went in to rescue his communion plate and
sacred relics. We came back along a river, and
for an hour or two we were walking in Belgium,
I believe , the fleets of barges seem to have been
sunk, but our engineers had rebuilt the broken
bridges on pontoons, and I saw one happy party,
two Tommies and six small French children, rowing
down the river in a government pontoon. There
was a weir pool which looked very inviting for a
bathe, but a sentry warned us that the spot was
under close observation from the German lines, and
in the slack water above, the rows of dead dogs
and cats did not make us regret it.

It is a great pleasure to see something new,
even if it's quite a dull field or a squalid street ;
no doubt when you first arrive there seems a lot
to see, but you get so used to everything that your
eyes soon forget to take notice of what would
interest people at home.

Some big guns were firing on our right as we
walked back, making a horrid noise, and in return
the Germans were bursting heavy shrapnel and
high explosives over the roofs of a village. It's
queer to see the great puff of black smoke suddenly
spread in the sunshine and melt away before the
report of the explosion reaches you. I saw one
great factory-shed full of bales of wool, which
had been arranged to make cover inside against

shell fire ; I think nothing could be better. The chimney stack had had a piece bitten out of its side by a shell, but, strange to say, it was still standing.

We had the pipes playing in mess last night ; we always do one night in billets, and then the pipe-major comes in and takes a glass of port from the colonel and drinks the regimental toast in Gaelic, which I can't attempt to write down, but which means ' Highlanders, shoulder to shoulder.' It's a little ceremony which always pleases me. Sometimes, too, the pipers march up and down the village street in the evening, playing for all they are worth ; last night it was ' The Barren Rocks of Aden,' which is a familiar tune at home, but seems to mean much more when you hear it out in France, perhaps because it was written for Scotsmen far from Scotland. I believe the Brittany regiments sometimes have a kind of bagpipe too, which they call ' binion.'

I could not help smiling just now when I came into my billet, and found the poor old priest tilted back helpless in his chair, his brow showing pale as parchment above a lather of soap, while a fat, red, jolly barber waved a razor round his head, and seized him by the nose. I woke the other morning to hear his bell ringing for his morning mass. I don't know what the reason is for ringing a bell at their sacrament ; probably it was meant to drive away evil spirits.

I was afraid that I should have to go digging to-night, but now it seems they don't want anybody ; it always falls to someone in this company, because two platoons are in disgrace for killing hens in the farm where they are billeted. I came out of mess about 10 o'clock one very dark night, and was met by a flustered corporal who said, ' Beg yer pardon, sir, but they're throwing deid cocks and hens in among us,' and so they were, and next morning there were nine victims laid out, and one already half cooked, but in the dark the culprits escaped and have never owned up. Of course it was very wrong, but I expect the hens were roosting up in the rafters above their heads, and making themselves unpleasant guests, and I don't think it was real looting. Anyway, the two platoons will dig until further orders.

I will put some photos in this letter from B.C. and Edgehill, please keep them for my book, and this other letter might interest you ; I had suggested casually that when the peace comes they might make a great road, all along the line of this western front, with a broad strip of ground on either side well planted with fruit trees and trees for shade. It would be a useful war memorial, for a great road is always useful. It might be made most beautiful too, besides being the most interesting road in the world for future generations of Englishmen and Frenchmen.

When I was in Washington I was so much impressed with the cemetery at Arlington on the far side of the Potomac, where lie 16,000 soldiers from the Northern armies who fought to free America from slavery, and it seems not unfitting that they should be buried there round the home of General Lee, who was such a marvellous general on the Southern side, and such a fine man too ; just as honestly convinced that in fighting for State rights and Virginia he was fighting for liberty. It's not in the least a morbid place like most cemeteries, but a beautiful garden which, from its character, is more than a public park can ever be.

Billets : July 11, 1915.

This has been a black day for me ever since I saw Bay Balfour's[1] name in the lists from the Dardanelles. I can remember him so well as I first saw him, on that hot July day outside school at Winchester, before he and I went in to do our papers at the same table. We went up the school together all the way, and he was always the life of every class. And at Oxford I came to know him even

[1] 2nd Lieut. Isaac Bayley Balfour, attached 1st K.O.S.B., son of Professor Bayley Balfour of Edinburgh.

better, until latterly he was in many ways my greatest friend. He was the most lovable of men— so lively and full of zest and joy in living that he made all his friends feel glad to be alive. ·

He had a strong character too, with all his charm—for all his popularity at school left him quite unspoilt. He managed his house splendidly, and whatever he decided to do, he would have done well ; but he never could have painted a better picture than his own five and twenty years, for there is nothing in them that any of his friends would ever wish to forget   I have written to Mrs. Balfour, but didn't know what to say ; he was the sunshine of that house.

If only we could have done our training this last winter together—somehow I was afraid that I should never see him again.

This is no letter, but I can think of nothing but Bay Balfour.

Billets . July 13, 1915

I am back in the old bit of trench which I first held when I came out in February, but what a difference between then and now ; the men used to be huddled together on little islands, built up with sand-bags, over what was left of the old trench in front. Machine-guns used to play on us most of the night, and the sniper flicked earth down from the parapet all day. It was the favourite corner for shells too. Now, an hour often passes with hardly a shot fired, we walk up and down in safety behind a good solid breastwork; in fact, you could probably walk all the way along the line to La Bassée. The ground is as hard as a brick and as dry as a bone, and it wasn't till I dug a bit of new trench yesterday that the smell reminded me of the place where I had floated a hurdle on rotten cabbage stalks in a sea of mud, to try to make a moderately dry crossing over a bottomless pit. No wonder the men ask anxiously whether we expect to be here another winter. Probably you know more about that at home than we do.

These five days Bankier and I are attached to another company; the Captain is a very nice fellow, and it's quite pleasant for a change to live in a different mess, but for the time everything is stale and flat to me, since I heard of Bay Balfour's death. I have always been very lucky to have so many friends, and lucky too in this war, since Stainton, Wilson, and Fowler have all been very badly wounded, but are recovering; but there was never anyone quite like Bay Balfour. At school he had so many friends in his own house that I didn't know him better than many others, but lately I knew him as well as anyone, perhaps better.

Ralph Fowler's letters were very interesting; he's a lucky man, for if it had been cold weather, or if he had had to lie in a wet trench with that wound, he would never have recovered.

(*July* 15.) This letter was never taken up, so I will add a piece to it.

Just to spite me for saying it was so different from February, we had very heavy rain last night, which in a few hours created quagmires and sloughs of despond wherever feet churned the mud up; that's the worst of this country, it's so flat that there's nowhere for water to drain away, and as soon as you dig below the surface at all, the water gathers and the clay holds it, so that it takes a long time to soak in. Luckily it cleared off at 1 A.M, and to-day I could have caught a sea trout I know, for there is a fine fresh breeze from the south-west and a cloudy sky. I'm glad of wind again; though we often curse the winds at home, we miss them out here.

I still think we shall get through the Dardanelles, but it is difficult to see how we are to reach a decision on this western front; but if we feel the strain in our factories at home, and suffer from the long casualty lists, what must it be in Germany, where Prussia, with a smaller population than ourselves, has a list five times as heavy?

The world is a poorer place without Tom and

Bay Balfour, and I do feel that, if it wasn't for all of you at home, I should be quite content to follow them. If 'getting used to it' means that one slowly forgets how much there was to love in them, I would rather keep the pain for ever. Perhaps Daisy would show you some verses I wrote about Bay Balfour; afterwards I worked at them until I made them rather better, but still not nearly good enough.

Trenches : July 15, 1915.

Yes, I remember writing some lines about the walk back from Rackwick, one night at Oxford when I could not sleep. I thought I had torn them up, and I'm sure they are not worth sending to the *Spectator*, but if you like, send them to me, and I will have a look at them, for I have forgotten all except the beginning and the end, of which you remind me. . . . Latin and Greek lend themselves to epitaphs almost better than English. . . . I've often tried to write about Tom, but somehow I never could. The better you know people, the less easy it is to write about them. No one can give any real reasons why he likes his brothers and sisters—the feeling is there, and that's all about it. I can always write verses if I set myself to it, but as a rule I'm too lazy, for it usually costs me a night's sleep; but writing real poetry is another matter; if you're a poet, the poems come of themselves, if not, no amount of labour will change your verses into poetry. I'm afraid the vicar's daughter was more a joke than a reality, and I've heard nothing of ministering spirits. In fact, after seeing how often the men write things in their letters which are pure imagination, I get rather sceptical about everything which I have not seen with my own eyes. I suppose some people would say I had no faith, because I never expect to see anything supernatural. (I remember in the autumn of 1899, when you took Gwen and me to Mull, we used to climb in the woods behind, with Tina and Kenneth and some other children, I think; and one day some of us thought that we saw fairies, and Gwen, as you would expect somehow, saw at least twice as many fairies as anybody else, and described them wonderfully; and I remember getting quite angry because I never could see anything at all, and when I did, it turned out to be a rabbit. Afterwards Gwen confessed, with tears, I think, that some of the fairies, at anyrate, were imaginary.) But it seems to me that this expectation of miracles is all part of that looking for a sign which Christ denounced. . . .

Billets : July 17, 1915.

We are moving off to-morrow, thank goodness ; it will be a relief to see something new. I enclose a lot of photos which Bankier took some months ago ; the prints have only just arrived, but they are very good indeed, only it's unfortunate that Clark has moved in the picture of him and me outside Company Headquarters and that stains have spoilt the one of Bankier and me shaving. What a pity that cameras are still taboo ! There is such a lot that could not give anything to the Germans, but would make most fascinating pictures. . . . I saw Sholto this afternoon, looking enormous as usual ; he seems to like the 91st, and his company commander especially ; we are not likely to meet again for some time. I never saw a billet like this for flies ; they hang in great black clusters on the walls like swarming bees ; fly-papers get covered two or three deep in half an hour ; we are trying poison too, but however we may ' strafe ' there are just as many left. Our company have held an impromptu concert, which wound up with a song from me and ' wee doch-an-dorris ' from Bankier—great enthusiasm. I bet half of them try to fall out on the march, for their feet are as soft as butter after all these months.

Billets : July 21, 1915.

I have enjoyed these last two days, in a curious sort of way, as much as any since I came out. We marched off from our old billets about 2 o'clock yesterday—not sorry to see the last of them. For, though our last two days there were spent in a farm a good way farther back, we were still in the middle of the same fields, and still within reach of shells, if any had happened to come. It was a clear, sunny day, with a breeze from the west, and the country was still fresh after last week's rain. My company was second in the line, so that we could hardly hear the pipes at the head ; but the men were pleased to be on the move again, and marched well in spite of the heat. At first we came back along the same road which I travelled five months ago in February, when I marched up with the draft. It was very different now ; the low ground which had all been flooded was dry, and the mud was gone. The traffic on the road was much the same—A S C motor lorries, ambulances, and staff officers' cars. In one place we passed an armoured car, mounting machine-guns which had broken down. A little later on, everyone was called to attention—that is always done when we pass a guard—and when I gave ' eyes left,' there was an Indian trooper, in turban, and baggy trousers,

R

rigid as a poker, with an enormous sabre, very broad, and curved in the blade, held straight up in front of him. It was very difficult not to laugh, and some of the men who had been in India called out to him in Hindustani, but he looked neither to right nor left, and as if his life depended on keeping his eyes on the blade. We only came about eight miles, and then billeted in different farms; but the country is different, for there are tall edges, like the English hedges, instead of those bare fields— the wheat is turning yellow, and the farms are still inhabited. It's a pleasure to see them without gaps in the walls or roof, and with all their live-stock and animals. For the Germans pushed through this district very quickly in October, and had only time to fire the churches as they passed; possibly our own artillery did some of the damage, for the Germans used to mount machine-guns in the towers to cover their retreat. I am by myself with two platoons in a small farm—the farmer and his family are all very friendly, and press me to have coffee with them, whenever I pass out and in to my room. I sleep on a table, and I don't mind a hard surface in the least, if it isn't uneven; and besides, as I told the farmer, it is better to sleep *on* the table than to sleep underneath it. He was very much pleased when I explained the joke, and has been offering me wine and beer ever since. One of his sons has been called out, but is not yet 'sur le front.' He had never had *Écossais* here before, only English and Canadians. He showed me the place where he hid, with his two sons, when the Germans came through, a little hole under the roof; but they did very little damage here. I made several other friends when I went to look for other billets; we had too little room at first, and one old farmer was so delighted to see my kilt that he seized my hand and shook it for a couple of minutes. He was very anxious to put me up, but he had already a full company of 250 men in his farm, so that we could not go there. He told me that he was seventy-six, had eleven children, and some incredible number of grandchildren, of whom the latest were twins; most of them seemed to live under his roof, and also two nieces who had fled from Lille. He himself had fought in 1870, but he still works away in the fields I must go and see him again. To-day we have done nothing; we may move off to new trenches in a couple of days, or we may be here a week, for we are now attached to another division. It was a bright, sunny day again, still with the same fresh breeze, and I had a walk with the doctor —there are some hills not far away, beyond the rail-head from which I marched in February, and there is an observation balloon hanging over a park for aeroplanes. Our sentry counted forty of them all going off early this morning on some raid, flying quite low. . . .

Billets : July 22, 1915.

I have been asleep on my table all the afternoon, a different method of resting from yesterday's, when I walked about four miles into a town, and saw the sights, such as they are—an old town hall, a fine church tower, spoilt with a thimble of modern brick on the top of it, a great many motor lorries driven by A.S.C., a good many padres, and almost the same number of French barmaids, wearing the badges of their favourite regiments. I even saw a train, the first for five months. We found a path through the fields for part of the way, which saved us from the *pavé*—wheat fields, for the most part, just turning yellow, rows of pollard willows showing silver in the wind, red-roofed farms, and one or two unbattered church spires in the distance—very peaceful and pastoral. I wish now that I had walked farther, for the day was very clear though sunny, and Ramsay, who rode to a hill just five miles farther on, was able to see Ypres in the distance, and shells bursting over it. I would have tried to get there to-day, but the day was dull, and so I slept. This

morning we were inspected by the General
commanding the 3rd Corps ; he kept us waiting
for over an hour, which was very annoying of him,
but when he did come, he was very pleasant and
complimentary. We may go back to the trenches
to-morrow night, but it is not settled yet. . . .
The South Wales miners will probably find plenty
of people to tell them that they were true patriots,
victims of an unfortunate misunderstanding, and
so forth. At the best, their case was that they
wanted a greater share in the spoil, and at the
worst, something very mean indeed. However, it's
over now. If leave is not stopped again, I shall
probably get home for a few days in September,
but I'm afraid that there is every likelihood that
it will be stopped before then ; this front has been
quiet for so long that something must happen
soon. . . .

Billets : July 23, 1915.

We are marching back to the trenches to-day,
in a different place, about eight miles away, I think,
so that we shall not have a long march. I shall
be quite sorry to leave this place, for it was restful.
We could hardly hear the guns at all, or see the
flares at night. Last evening I walked to a village
near ; there was very little to see except a large

church which had been burnt. In the square beside it was a whole supply train of motor lorries, nearly one hundred of them I suppose, all filled with stores, and ready to move off. You wondered how on earth armies managed to feed themselves before the day of the motor, and still more before the railways came. I am sending you some more photos. These are duplicates of some I sent before, which perhaps Gwen would like to see ; it is some time since I heard of her, but I suppose the mails are still irregular. I think the whole course of the Welsh strike has been disgraceful ; the Welsh coal-masters managed things very badly, but that was no excuse for the men ; plenty of M.P.'s would have seen to it that they got full justice if they had stuck to their work, while setting out their grievances. It's more and more clear to me that we shall need some system of conscription to carry on this war through the winter. For one thing the Expeditionary Force will lose between twenty and thirty thousand reservists this autumn, whose time was up nearly a year ago, but who were bound by the terms of enlistment to serve another year in time of war. They are just as patriotic as other men, but having been out here a year, they feel that they would like a turn at home, with high wages and a comfortable house, and one day in seven clear even when the pressure of work on ammunitions, &c.

is greatest ; and until it's made clear that every available fighting man is wanted in the field, one can't blame them. To a Frenchman, of course, the idea of letting a trained soldier go in time of war would seem quite ridiculous, but it will have to be done unless we change our system ; and it's not enough to make an army order forbidding them to go, for that would leave them with a genuine grievance. . . .

Trenches : July 25, 1915.

Many happy returns of your birthday, I'm glad to think you will spend it at Rhuveag, and I hope you will have a tea-picnic to celebrate it. I was just thinking that I had no present to give you, and behold a present has been provided, for this morning I was pulling down my dug-out, a very poor one, which had been half knocked in by a shell before I came to it. In a corner underneath some rubbish, I found a pouch for revolver ammunition, left there by some officer, and in it, besides some cartridges, was a cigarette holder, and this gold ring ; at least it seems to be 9-carat gold, and an Irishman in my platoon swears that he has sold many rings, and that this is genuine. I wonder what its history can be—had his lady hardened her heart and jilted him for one of Kitchener's army ?

or did it belong to a French girl ? or was it destined for someone before he left home, and never presented ? Anyway it shall be yours now. . . . There's nothing very striking about it except its strange history, but I think the emerald is genuine.

We came back into trenches two nights ago. We left our corn-fields and farms about 4 o'clock, and marched five miles first of all, over a bridge broken and repaired, and past a church, ruined and gutted by fire as usual. It was *pavé* most of the way, but a fresh summer afternoon. Then we all halted in a large field, where the men had their tea from our travelling kitchens, and we ourselves went on a little farther, to a cross-roads, where the forces of good and evil were drawn up facing one another—an *estaminet* on the one side, and the priest's house on the other. We had tea in the latter ; the reverend gentleman was gone, but he had left his clerical furnishings behind him, portraits of His Holiness the Pope, and of his own family, his sisters mostly nuns, and his brothers priests like himself. We marched on at dusk, down a long straight road with farms on either side, which gradually became more battered and deserted as we came nearer the firing line, and, finally, we had a laborious half-mile through a very narrow winding communication trench, where you had in places to turn sideways to prevent the pack on your shoulders from sticking fast ; subalterns usually carry packs and equipment just like the men now. We found some very nervous Territorials in our trenches, their first experience, and they had been shelled heavily one evening. I think it just as well the Germans had not attacked, for I don't think many of their sentries dared to look over the parapet even at night. As a rule, the Territorials are now just as good as any other troops, but these had left the trench in a terrible mess, and we have been cleaning up ever since. We are about 150 yards from the Germans ; we blew up a mine underneath their parapet some weeks ago, which hustled them a bit, but otherwise I think this trench has been an island of comparative rest, though some of the bloodiest fighting in the war took place on either side. It's very flat, low meadow-land, with tall, waving grass, and rows of pollard willow stumps, a regular swamp in winter I should think, and even now a deep trench would gather water in the bottom, and the weather has been broken lately. Almost every regiment in the British Army seems to have been here in turn— Scots Guards, Devons, Irish Rifles, Lancashire Fusiliers, Cameronians, Royal Scots ; you can see their wooden crosses standing here and there among the grass. Last night I was patrolling out in front, and actually saw a lot of Germans working on their parapet, and also a patrol who came within 30 yards of us. Two of them stayed beside a tree, and we lay there for a couple of hours, just about 20 yards away, waiting for clouds to come across the moon, for it was too bright to go forward or back. I hoped the two of them would come forward, for then the two of us would probably have made one a prisoner ; but perhaps they spotted us, for they fired two shots, and after that never moved. We were so close to the German trenches that I could smell the smoke of a German cigar— quite a good one too—not poisonous gas.

The photos came last night ; some of them might have been clearer, but they are not bad, and I shall want a lot of prints presently. The *Round Table*, F. S. Oliver's book, and one or two other things have also come ; thank you very much for them. . . . This letter may be too late now to reach you on your birthday, but anyway it will take you my love.

Trenches : July 28, 1915.

We are still hard at work strengthening and improving these trenches, and there is enough to keep us busy for a long time. Last night our old friend the sausage bomb made a reappearance— he came flying over my platoon into the next

company, but did no damage. Again about midnight they sent out three or four of them ; they
have a train of sparks flying from their tails at
night, so you can just see them coming. We have
taken to pieces two which failed to explode ; there
is nothing inside them except the powder, which
looks curiously like wet yellow sand, and smells
like almond paste. The next brigade made a
good deal of noise firing on a German working
party, so their guns opened on us, but they only
sent a few shells, and the first seemed to burst
in their own trench, and the next two in their own
wire, so the Germans are not always perfect, and
I expect someone will be 'strafed' for it. It's
sunny, windy weather, with occasional showers,
not very hot, in fact not so hot as it was at the
end of May. I hope you will get some trout out
of the loch I rather fancy that shore round the
sandy point on the far side of Loch Doine, though
I can't say I ever got much there. How splendid
that Eric Colbourne got the Military Cross, and
though it's hard that he should not have lived to
wear it, Florence will be proud to have it ; and
it must have been a very gallant bit of work ; he
did a lot in his three weeks at the front, though
the time seemed short . . .

Trenches : (possibly a day earlier than above).

Last night I took three men with bombs, and we got right up to the German wire. I have cut a specimen of it, which I shall send home as a souvenir, unless the Brigade Staff want it. We brought in a curious iron stake, which the Germans use for rigging up their barbed wire, made in one piece out of an iron rod looped while the iron is hot, so that the wire can be just threaded through the loops, and it has a corkscrew end, so that it can be screwed into the ground noiselessly, just as you screw in the stake which anchors a tennis net, only, of course, this is much thinner and slighter. I don't think it's stout enough to be of much use, but it's an interesting thing, and Major Hyslop, who is commanding while Colonel Gore is home on leave, sent down a message this morning to congratulate me, so I feel quite pleased, for of course information about their wire is useful. . . . We are likely to be in the trenches for two days more, I think. A sprig of bog-myrtle from Mother this morning which still smells very sweet. . . .

Trenches : July 29, 1915.

We have had another quiet day except for a few sausages ; however this evening we managed to mark the spot from which they were coming and put a rifle grenade right into it, which shut them up. The sun was very hot to-day after a cold moonlit night. Our knees are all getting very sunburnt. To-night we go back into billets, two or three miles to march I expect, but it's worth it to get well away from shells. . . .

You might send me some time a copy of the W.O.'s description of the place where Tom was buried ; I am nowhere near it at present, but some day, if we were to move, I might find myself within reach of it. I think you said it was accurately described to you. I don't think it matters very much though where and how anyone is buried. . .

Billets   July 30, 1915

. . . I see Mai thinks I have a sunny temperament ; she would not get the same opinion from some of my men. I have been biting their heads off lately ; too many flies, too little sleep, and too much work in a hot sun to keep a philosophic mind, and the men themselves get lazy, and want to spend their time grousing about the state in which their trenches have been left, instead of getting to work to put them right. Of course they do have some hardships out here, but take it all round, we are very well treated, almost too well ; when I see piles of bully beef tins going to waste, and fires made up with biscuit, it makes me quite mad, and I just wish we could all change places with the French for six months, and see what it means to be fighting, with half your own country in ruins, on a half-penny a day, and just enough food to keep going, while perhaps you left your family behind in Lille, and haven't heard of them for ten months.

It's one disadvantage of our voluntary system that the press and every one else try to persuade officers and men that they are little heroes to have come out here at all, and that they deserve the best of everything; whereas they are just doing what every Frenchman has got to do as a matter of course. I'm for encouraging the men in a tight place, and for keeping them as busy as possible at all other times. There's just a bit too much sitting still, and not firing at the Germans because it will only make them fire back; but we should always fire when there is any target, and take jolly good care to aim straighter; it's the only way to end the war, and we know that when we take the trouble we can always give them more than we get.

The Russians seem to have checked the Germans for the time, but it will be a hard task to hold that salient with the Germans pressing in from three sides. I don't know more than anyone else why we are waiting so long for the next move on this front, but there must be some good reason.

I have been sleeping this afternoon, so far as the flies would let me, and listening in the intervals to flirtations in broken English, and still more broken French, between the men and the dairymaids at the farm. The French all seem to like *les Écossais* better than the English regiments ; they come back to their houses sometimes if they hear a Scotch regiment is coming there.

I see Tom Erskine of the 4th Battalion is killed ; he was one of the nicest of the Glasgow O.T.C. men, very competent and a keen soldier ; his name was in the list with Eric Colbourne's for the Military Cross, and he seemed to have deserved it most thoroughly. That's the worst of this damnable war ; it just lops off the bravest men as you might lop off the tallest heads of bracken with your stick, and once a man gets a reputation for keeping his head, and doing difficult jobs, he's bound to be picked for them. However it's a fine life out here, and if I come through I shall never regret the time spent in the trenches ; one can't call them ' crowded hours,' but they are as well spent as most in peace time.

Billets : August 1, 1915.

The weather has turned very hot again. July was really a cold month out here, and very showery, but now we are getting harvest weather. I grudge the Germans Warsaw very much ; of course Napoleon got Moscow, and suffered more than gained by it, and whether they hold Warsaw or not, the Russians will go on fighting ; but still it will encourage the Germans very much for their autumn campaign. There are a good many Indian troops near here. I walked along the river this morning, and saw them bathing and washing themselves, and leading their horses down to water. Some of them were splendid looking men, very tall, with great turbans and long black beards ; they are fighting very well now when they get a chance in the open, but this trench warfare doesn't suit them ; they can't understand what prevents them from charging across to the German lines, and if they try it, there are none left with experience to warn the others. It's not a question of bravery, but simply a mathematical certainty that, in the face of so many bullets, no man can escape being hit, unless the guns have just demoralised the enemy, and broken up their trenches.

I marched a large party to the baths this afternoon, very hot and dusty, but our piper played the whole way without stopping. The French people are still very much interested in a Highland regiment, though, of course, it's nothing new to them now, for all the Scottish regiments are particularly strong in Territorial as well as line battalions. The English regiments are jealous and make rude remarks about the pipes, but a mouth organ is a miserable instrument compared with them. I don't see why they shouldn't have full military bands out here ; it would cheer everyone up when we are back in billets. There is so little for the men to do except eat and sleep, and try to get more beer than they are allowed from the *estaminets*. So flame or liquid fire is the latest German device. They won't stop the war with all these infamous weapons, but they will make their name loathed for evermore, until they repudiate the Great General Staff which approves of such things Some people say, why observe rules in war, since it seems an artificial distinction to kill by one weapon, and not to allow some other ; but war at the best is a bloody business, and it's only by sticking to the few rules that men have agreed to keep, that we can prevent ourselves from descending lower than beasts ; fighting like the two devils in the ' Inferno ' who fell back into the lake of pitch biting and tearing one another with their nails.

S

This day last year I remember I spent going
down to Salisbury Plain with the Inns of Court
squadron ; unboxing horses, and putting up tents ;
then in the evening, after ten minutes' sleep, we
were all roused up to move straight back to London
—and the great game began.   It was all very exciting
in those days ; somehow, now that I am in the
middle of it, I have lost the sense of tremendous
happenings which I had then ; and I was much
more anxious when I put my name in for a commission in the Special Reserve, which Mitchison
and I did among the first few volunteers, than I
am now when I go back to the trenches.   To-day
we have had cloud and sun with heavy showers.
I walked into the local village to have my hair
cut, and waited for an age in a very hot room with
nothing to read except some newsless French news-
papers, and an advertisement, with specimens, of
some man's art in working portraits with human
hair ; rather an unpleasant art, I think.   There
were a great many Indians in the streets ; most
of them wear big khaki turbans with a touch of
red in them, and the cavalry have little epaulettes
of dark chain mail.   They are very fine-looking
men ; the Indians have never had a proper chance
yet to show what they can do, but they sit patiently

beside the river, grooming or watering their horses, or squat in little groups round their cooking-pots. I always thought Falkirk had more public-houses than any other place, but I believe this little town could beat it in *estaminets*. They have all sorts of titles; perhaps 'Au Retour de l'Abattoir' was the most unpleasant, and 'Aux Vainqueurs de Paris' the most curious. I suppose it refers to the Marseillais who marched to Paris in 1789. They must be funny little places in peace time, these French towns. Our *estaminet* was called 'Réunion des Sapeurs-Pompiers,' which means, I think, the fire-brigade; no doubt they were great people in full uniform, and how indignant they must be now that uniforms have become so cheap! . . . I was afraid I should be sent digging to-night, but luckily I have escaped. We have never got any more captains since these three were knocked over, only one second lieutenant.

What shall we do if I get a week's leave in September? You must not count upon it, because very likely leave will be stopped again.

Billets: August 3, 1915.

Here there is 'nothing to report'; it seems likely that we shall be in billets longer than usual, and that, when we do go back, we shall have more

s 2

of Kitchener's Army with us for instruction. It's a very long time now since there was any real fighting on the British front, a trench taken here and there, but no serious attacks on either side. I had a walk to-day along flat, straight roads among the corn-fields; there is a great deal of wheat round here, and they were reaping it by hand. I had a chat with a French boy who was busy with his scythe; he said 'les Écossais sont meilleurs soldats que les Anglais, parcequ'ils sont plus chauds—comme les Français.' I don't know whether it was his own idea, or picked up from a newspaper. Last winter some people said the exact opposite, that the English regiments were doing best in this war, because they didn't get impatient while sitting in the trenches. I see in to-day's paper that A. G. Heath has been wounded, I hope not seriously; somehow I seem to last longer than all my friends; they all get killed or wounded, one after another, as soon as they come out. . . .

We never get any news of Clark, but I hope he is round the corner now. What a vast difference that half-inch either way does make. It seems so petty that a miserable little thing like a modern bullet can come along and make waste of the whole marvellous machine, so quickly too, when a tree the man has planted the day before may go on living for a hundred years. I wonder what the

Navy is thinking about, with all these preparations; they usually keep their secrets better than the Army, I think; perhaps because there are fewer in the secret. Here everything seems to be the talk of every pot-house for days before it happens; the only great exception was Neuve Chapelle; and even then we knew something, and the troops in that part of the line must have known more. But often it seems to me that orders are published far too early and too widely. I prefer Stonewall Jackson's plan, of putting his whole army into a train, so that not a soul knew which way they were going to start. Yet the crossing of the original force, and the movement from the Aisne to the Northern frontier were managed very well and very quietly. There's so little to talk about in this trench warfare, that when people do get wind of a piece of news, they seem compelled to chatter about it. . . . .

Billets   August 4, 1915

This morning we should have had one of those small Lammas floods, which make such good fishing, for there was heavy rain part of the night. I remember two floods like that in the very *dry* August of our first year at Glencaird, which Mother will remember too. They have begun the harvest here ; they hardly seem to use machinery at all, but do all their reaping with a small scythe-sickle, about two feet long, and a short pole with an iron hook on it, for gathering the sheaf together and holding it while it is cut ; they manage to lay the sheaves very neatly in rows, and work quite fast, cutting with one hand and gathering with the other. I was talking to a French boy of sixteen or so yesterday ; his scythe, I was interested to see, was made in Germany, but his hone was British made ; yet I'm sure Sheffield could turn out the scythes just as well, if we would take our chance of getting the market now. He told me he could make ten francs a day while the harvest lasted, working from 5 in the morning till 8 at night, a long day, but not a bad wage for a boy. By all the laws of economics it ought to pay them better to buy reaping-machines, for the fields are large and the ground as level as can be ; but, of course, the farms are smaller than at home, and the people work so hard that I think they make more out of them than we should. His father and brother were both away serving in the French army. . . . I suppose the Russians are desperately short of ammunition, for rifles as well as artillery. But they won't give in, and the effort of pushing into their country will be most exhausting for the Germans. . . . When you send out those photos, send them in an ordinary parcel, otherwise the censor might think I had been taking photos these last three months, which, of course, I have not done, and it would take a lot of correspondence to explain that they were old prints ; the rule about cameras is very strict now. . . . Our doctor is leaving to go back to the London Hospital, and I shall miss him very much. Bankier has also left the company to act as adjutant. I'm very glad he has got the job ; he was the best man for it, and others seemed at one time more likely to have it. So now I have one of the Clan Campbell for my company commander, and a new subaltern who got his commission from the 9th H.L.I. Glasgow Highlanders. The colonel came back from leave yesterday. It appears that my iron corkscrew stake was the first of its kind brought in, so they were glad to have it ; although I think others have been brought in in several places since. . . .

Billets · August 6, 1915.

I am writing from a very comfortable billet ; a villa belonging to a French officer, formerly commandant des Sapeurs-Pompiers in this little town. But the fire-brigade are now themselves extinguished, and M. le Commandant, who lost an arm early in the war, is training cadets in some

other part of France. So we sit on his chairs and
sofa, admire ourselves in his long mirrors, and
marvel at his taste in decorations. The mantel-
piece in the sitting-room, for instance, has three
small marble busts on it, in imitation of the classical
styles, but beside these ladies, or rather among
them, are a large brown stoat and a small white
weasel, while facing one another, like West and
East, are a cock-pheasant and a golden pheasant.
In the dining-room next door, there are mountain
scenes painted on the panels, while above the fireplace, two barn owls with outstretched wings, are
roosting on long poles, and a great grey shrike
sits disconsolately among the fly-papers which are
hanging from the chandelier. I don't know that
I wish to see owls in the dining-room any more
than bats in the attic, but there they are. These
materials don't help us very far in guessing what
the commandant is like ; it's always a fascinating
game to try and reconstruct people from their
belongings, but from his library I gather that he
was a Royalist. Royalism used to be strong in this
corner of France, I think, they are so intensely
Catholic ; but if the French Republic and its army
come through this war successfully together, I
fancy Royalism is dead ; before, there was always
a chance that the army would quarrel with the
politicians and choose its own leader. The com-

mandant has a fine garden full of pears, which should be ripe next month, and he had a fine cellar, but the Welsh Fusiliers bought the last of it from his housekeeper last week. This town must have been a very quiet, peaceful little place before the war ; curiously enough the regiment billeted here on October 20 last year, just before the heaviest fighting in the advance, when it was still untouched ; and it has not suffered very much except in the corner beside the church, which has been wrecked, and the houses beside it levelled with the ground. There is rather a pretty old garden behind it, which must, I think, have belonged to the church, or to some establishment of clerics. Their house is no more, for it was in line with the church tower, but the roses in their garden are in bloom and very sweet. There is a pond too, with some pale goldfish in it, which seemed to have a great fondness for the mud at the bottom, in which they buried themselves entirely. I could not understand this, until I saw a kingfisher fly away from the pond as I came near it this morning. No doubt he will stay there as long as there are any goldfish left. The garden will very soon be a wilderness. I never knew what a fine flower spinach (endive ?) has, until I saw it there run to seed ; there is a smaller walled garden with vines all round the walls, masses of bright green, pear trees, and those small French

strawberries, half-way between the wild straw-
berry and the garden kind. All this place is 'out
of bounds ' to the troops, for it must be an unhealthy
corner when shells are falling; the biggest shell-
holes I have seen in France are there, one at least
20 feet across. The bottom was full of water,
and the frogs had just accepted it as the gift from
heaven of a fine new pond. We go back into the
trenches to-night; these eight days out are the
longest holiday I have had since February, and of
course we have been drilling and marching at times.
We shall have some Rifle Brigade from Kitchener's
Army in with us for instruction.

Reserve Billets : August 7, 1915.

I am likely to have an easy time of it these
six days, for B company is not in the firing line at
all, being divided between some fortified points,
and a ruined farm, which holds two platoons and
myself and Alastair Campbell; unless they shell
us, we shall live and sleep in peace. There are
orchards all round about, and the men are throwing
sticks and stones at the hard green apples and
pears, and if it were not for the holes in all the
roofs and walls, you would think you were miles
from the firing line. This morning I took a digging
party to work on a communication trench; it's

not often you can dig by daylight. As I wandered round, while the men were busy, I suddenly came upon young Gladstone's grave,[1] in the corner of an orchard railed off, where he lies with about fifty men of different regiments—Gordons, Wiltshires, Royal Scots, Irish Rifles, and Welsh Fusiliers, it's curious to think of him there and his grandfather in Westminster Abbey; but they are both in honourable company.

The country is all of the same pattern—farms more or less ruined with orchards round them, rows of poplars and willows, and wide fields where the long grass of May is already bleached and withering; there don't seem to be pigeons or other birds to harvest the corn which sowed itself and is now overripe. It all seemed rather melancholy to me, perhaps because I knew that one of our biggest efforts in the war had been made across that stretch of ground. I could see the empty gun-emplacements everywhere, and the trenches in rows one behind another where the supports waited for the chance which never came; for somehow or other things went wrong and the attack was a failure. In some places they were just mown down by the German machine-guns as soon as they tried to leave their trenches, and elsewhere they got to the German wire, only to find it still uncut,

[1] The body has since been removed to Hawarden.

and the few companies which did get through and into the German lines found themselves unsupported, and had to fall back ; no doubt the effort helped us or the French by drawing troops away from other hard pressed places, but it was very costly. I believe the dead are still lying thick out in front, just where they fell. However, I don't think such things are really depressing, for they just leave you with the determination to reward all these past efforts by success at last, and I never doubt myself that success is coming, though it may be long in coming.

I had a Canadian letter yesterday written from Georgian Bay. There is something very charming about those innumerable rocky islands, with their twisted pine trees and deep clear water in between, and the great sweep of Lake Huron to the west, as wide as the sea. You must go there some day.

I notice one or two flowers which are new to me, but mostly they are just the same ; that big blue flower, wild chickory, I think, is common here among the corn, and the white convolvulus is very common everywhere ; such a pretty thing I always think.

Now I must inspect rifles, ammunition, and gas helmets.

Reserve Billets : August 8, 1915.

There is very little news, except that we captured a German prisoner to-day. Two of our men had gone out in front to bury a corpse, and they came across two Germans who had apparently come out to rob the dead—dirty brutes, neither our men nor the Germans were armed, but one of the Germans bolted, so they jumped on the other one. I did not see him, but of course the men were fearfully pleased; he was taken to the Colonel who gave him a meal of German sausage, and sent him on to the Brigade, with the note, ' Herewith one German prisoner, please send receipt.' There is a very handsome willow-herb which grows in the ditches here. I will get some seed if I can. It is more branched than our giant willow-herb, and the flowers grow closer together in spikes. Most of the flowers are just the same as at home. I saw the blue corn-flower growing wild to-day. I have had no letter for a day or two, but perhaps they will come in to-night. Last week our bomb subaltern went up to the river with a new kind of bomb and threw it in —result about twenty fish, one a big carp, the rest mostly roach and perch. . . . The Frenchmen seem to catch a good many, and our stretcher-bearers fish a lot too. We are starting to fish ourselves, so there will be no more poaching with bombs. . . .

August 9, 1915.

This has been a very hot sultry day, as I know to my cost, for I spent the morning with my platoon digging a new trench about half a mile behind the firing line. We were well screened from view, even from the captive balloon which was hanging in the air over the German lines as usual, like a great caterpillar; so that we could work by daylight, which is always more satisfactory. The men were working practically naked, and the only disadvantage was a very populous wasp's nest close beside the trench. I got stung twice on the knee, but either it is a very long time since I was stung, or these French wasps are not so venomous, for their stings don't bother you after five minutes. Some of the men were stung too, and were much more alarmed by the wasps in pursuit than by some shrapnel which the Germans put over just in front of us. They rattled a few apples and pears down off the trees in the orchard, smashed a dug-out, and hit a water-bottle, but did no real damage; and at present, in this part of the front, our heavy guns give them far more to think about every day than they give us: and our aeroplanes are busy every day watching for their batteries. I was digging till midnight last night too; a clear starry night, with a great many shooting stars.

The Bavarians opposite are rather nervous, I think, since they lost that prisoner to us, and we have also been annoying them in various ways; they kept on putting up flares, and opening bursts

of rapid fire, but they hit nothing. You get to
know the different sounds ; the crack of a rifle fire
straight in front is really the sound of the bullet
coming toward you all compressed into one sound ;
then there is the swishing sound of cross fire, and
the whee-er-ee of a ricochetting bullet. There
was heavy gun-fire to the north last night and
early this morning, and I hear that we have made
a successful attack   I am going off to-morrow to
Brigade Headquarters for a course in bomb throwing
—they are taking all subalterns for that one by one
—so for ten days I shall live in peace and comfort,
and probably sleep in a bed

Your letter came last night, as well as three
others, and the *Wykehamist*, so I did well by that
post   I see that a couple of lines of Greek, which
I had just scribbled at the bottom of the page,
have been printed along with my verses on Bay
Balfour—a famous epitaph of Plato on a friend
who died young, which plays on the contrast
between the morning and the evening star. Shelley
has translated it so far as I can remember—

Thou wast the morning star among the living
    Ere thy pure light had fled,
Now thou art gone, thou art as Hesperus giving
    New splendour to the dead.—

but the Greek is simpler and better.

I was interested in what you told me about

the Quarrier's orphan homes—how much better it is when these things can be done by private enterprise and not by Government, yet unless Government does them, they are so apt not to be done at all. . . .

Billets : August 12, 1915.

I prefer this 12th to last year's 12th, which I spent on Wimbledon Common, drilling on foot, on a boiling hot day, and there was just enough heather growing there to mock us.

To-day has been very hot, but I have spent it lying about on the grass watching the men throw their bombs, and being instructed in the theory and practice of working down trenches. It seems that we can usually beat the Germans at bombing; they can't throw so far, or so accurately. This evening I walked two or three miles to see the 1st Seaforths in the Bareilly Brigade, and found several 4th Battalion subalterns there; they have a fine-looking set of men, in spite of all their fighting, and they tell me that 90 per cent. of them are real Highlanders from Stornoway and Ross-shire; not so Highland as the 4th Battalion was, when I knew it, all the same.

I saw a great many Indians too—Gurkhas, Jats, and various others whose names I do not know;

they will be happy enough while the summer lasts, but I doubt whether they will put them in the trenches for another winter.

The war news from Gallipoli seems good, but it will take a lot of hard fighting yet.

I think now that I may get leave about the end of next week; I shall get about six days.

Billets : August 13, 1915.

How curious that Ronald's post-card[1] should only come now! That is just an example, I think, of German unpleasantness, deliberately refusing to do a kindness which would have relieved one family of anxiety. At least, I can't imagine that the post-card was delayed so long except by deliberate intention.

We have had another day of bomb-throwing; there is not very much to do while the men are just practising throwing, except sit and watch them; they are quite keen about it, and amused with the catapult which will throw a bomb over one hundred yards. We are rather scattered, for half the battalion are in billets and half in reserve in ruined farms behind the firing line.

[1] Written on January 10th by 2nd Lieut. R D. Gillespie, 2nd Gordon Highlanders, to say he had been taken prisoner on the 9th He, shortly after, made an attempt along with 2nd Lieut Gore-Browne to escape from Lille Citadel by jumping 40 feet. Mr Gore-Browne breaking his leg, they could go no farther, and were retaken.

T

Billets : August 15, 1915.

There was a little diversion for us yesterday—
a horse show for the division to which we are
attached. I was busy at the bomb school until
late in the afternoon, so that I was too late to see
anything, except the end of the jumping and the
wrestling on horse-back. Bankier and Campbell
were both disqualified early at the jumps, for their
horses refused, and I don't know who won, probably
some cavalry man; but the wrestling on horse-
back was very fierce, teams of four, stripped to
the waist, so as to be more slippery, and riding
bareback except for their bridles. The Middlesex
won after a tremendous tussle with the Royal
Irish Rifles, who fought like Kilkenny cats, but
were clawed off one by one, clawed literally, for
both sides were scratched and bleeding when they
finished, and they writhed and struggled till their
muscles stood out in knots; often they changed
horses in the middle, and climbed back again after
they seemed to be down, hanging on by their horses'
necks. The horses stood patiently, as if waiting
till their madness should have passed. There were
pipers and a band, and a great swarm of men and
horses and limbers in some open ground beside the
river, far back from the firing line. I never saw
so many red hats in my life, all the staff officers

from this part of the line and brigadiers as thick as blackberries. Many from the Indian Corps were there too. Those Indian Army officers are a regular type; keen wiry men most of them, with sunburnt faces and keen eyes puckered at the corners from much Indian sunshine; they must be fine soldiers, for I think they get the pick of Sandhurst year after year, and even in peace time their soldiering is much more strenuous out there.

I met a New College man, and yesterday a Wykehamist arrived here with a trench mortar battery; a friend of Tom's, both at Winchester and Oxford. He will be able to make it hot for the German trench mortar when he starts to work.

Your letter came yesterday and one from Gwen too; perhaps I shall be home for her birthday, but that is no good as she is not there.

Our bomb school came to an end this morning, for the brigade is moving to-day and to-morrow— back from the peaceful country we came from to go into these trenches—after that I don't know where we shall go, but I think we shall be absorbed into another division. I'm glad to move, for I always like a change, and if we can't move on, I'm always for moving sideways once a month, for I hate settling down, and I think it's bad for the men, though, of course, in some ways it's comfortable and easier. I'm glad to hear that Clark is better.

T 2

. . . I'm reading one of Dostoiefsky's novels, 'The Brothers Karamazov'—interesting, like all the Russians, but as I've only read 200 pages and there are 900 in the book, I've hardly begun. . . .

Billets : August 19, 1915, 9 A.M.

It seems hard to believe it, but to-night I shall be in England—for I have got my leave at last, until the 26th, so that I actually shall be at home on your birthday [1]—how I wish you could be there too !

At the moment I am sitting in an old farm-house—in a kitchen with an enormous fireplace and huge smoky rafters—and everything seems very quiet, for though it is only 7 o'clock, the regiment has marched off already.

I wish in a way that my leave had come some other time, for I like marching to new places, and to-day the brigade is to march past Lord Kitchener ; probably Sir J. French will be there too, and I should have liked to see them. Our brigade, which has been a sort of War Baby, nobody's child, after wandering about from one division to another, is now going to take the place of the Guards Brigade in the 2nd Division—and may be resting for some time. As a matter of fact, I have not been in the trenches for a fortnight, since, before we moved

[1] Written to his sister in Nairobi.

back, I was doing a course of bomb-throwing—
very important for all this fighting in trenches.

We marched back from our post near the firing
line by night—for a mile or two we kept the pipers
quiet, not so much from fear of rousing the Germans,
as of waking the General, but when we had passed
beyond his ears, the pipers blew for all they were
worth, the 'Earl of Maxwell' and other tunes,
whose names I never know though I can whistle
them. It was very weird somehow, marching along
in the middle of this tremendous war—the night
was dark, though starry, and there was a white
harvest mist rising from the low ground and stubbles.
Gradually the flares from the trenches grew fainter
behind us, as we went on past silent farms, and
through empty village streets, where the sound of
the pipes came echoing back from the walls.
Towards midnight the mist grew very thick; I could
see nothing except scattered trees looming up
suddenly from the fields, and the square shoulders
of my company commander riding his horse in front.
When the pipers stopped, it was very quiet except
for the steady tramp of 500 men. We billeted
some miles from the firing line, near where we lay
a month ago, an orchard and wheat-field country.

Yesterday I had a walk and a wonderful
view, for after six months I was able to find a hill
to climb—the Cats' Mountain—and from the

monastery at the top I could look down on the whole plain ; to the south and east it was rather hazy, so that I could hardly make out Lille and La Bassée, but to north and west I could see almost as far as Calais and Dunkirk—and Ypres lay below, across some miles of wooded hills and hop-fields, as pretty a stretch of country with its hops and corn-fields and woods and red roofs and church spires as you could wish to see, and although the trenches are so close in front, it seemed wonderfully unspoilt. A moving war tramples the country underfoot, but, except for the belt round the two lines of trenches, this waiting game does not do so much damage. I could see the ruined Cloth Hall at Ypres quite distinctly, and the ruined Cathedral Tower, and I could even see the shells bursting over Hooge—where we captured some trenches the other day—in puffs of white and black smoke. It was a marvellous sight, you might go there day after day for a week, and not get tired of it, and if ever I can go back there, I shall go—for on a clear day you could see beyond Arras to the south. The monastery has been turned into a convalescent hospital, a pleasant breezy place to lie, looking down across those miles of level country, with its villages and churches. I thought I heard the sound of monks chanting Mass, but when I came round the corner by the church, it was only six Tommies, dressed as pierrots, singing 'We pushed him through the window' to a large and happy audience of the patients. But some of the monks were there still, and I saw them bringing in their harvest, working in their long white robes, with cords round their waists. Some officers from the Indian Medical Corps gave me a 'hurl' down in their ambulance— which was lucky, for it was a good long walk, so long that, when I started, the others derided me and said I should never get there. But, in spite of six months in the trenches, I can still walk.

Friday, August 27, 1915.

I wrote this letter a week ago, and meant to finish it at home, and now here I am back at our billets, and I shall go into trenches this morning— it seems odd when I was in London only last night, as if both these worlds were not real. . . . On your birthday we rowed across the loch, climbed up to the gap above the fir-wood, then round the hill behind Stronvar, and back along the loch. A lot of grouse, and the heather smelt sweet, although there were showers

Billets : August 29, 1915.

It is a wonderful scene at Victoria when the leave train is starting to the front, but it must be much pleasanter to go with it than to stay behind when it is gone.

That Kentish country looked very green and sleepy and peaceful, and the Channel was very calm, with a bright full moon   We had one torpedo boat running alongside of us the whole way, and on the other side was a row of floats, from which I suppose the nets are hung; there didn't seem to be one continuous line all the way across, but no doubt they change the position of the nets constantly, like fishermen trying a fresh haul   The boat was crowded with officers of all ranks and services; and another new division has been crossing lately to Boulogne. I slept all the way up in the train, and reached my rail-head about five o'clock on a misty morning, then drove six or seven miles, quite pleasant after a night in the train, with the sun rising above the mist and corn-fields. The regiment was in trenches, with its transport back in this little village where we are now billeted, a slight ridge above some very low-lying ground. There is an old stone church, which seems to have escaped untouched for once, and some pretty villas, which I need hardly say are occupied by the artillery. I drove right up to the trenches by daylight in a gun limber, as noisy a drive as I have ever had in my life, for there were no springs, and the iron rimmed wheels rattled and banged on the *pavé*.

It was extemely hot, and in the distance I could see mine-heaps standing up everywhere through the haze ; for this is a mining district, and the French pile their waste into high pointed heaps, which are now used as observation posts by the artillery. It was through this part of the country that Tom marched and fought during his last few days, and later I saw roughly in the distance the place where he is buried. It must have looked very much the same to him, except that the leaves would be turning, and that the villages and farms would still be occupied and untouched. There are long straight paved roads, with plane trees planted on either side, wide fields of beetroot and corn and occasionally bits of wood, with châteaux we should almost call villas standing in them. By the way, what was the name of that château in which he slept ? I think you have a post-card of it. I may come across it, if it is not destroyed.

The line here has swayed to and fro with attacks and counter-attacks, so that the desert on either side is larger. There are some villages and factories just behind our trenches where hardly one stone is left upon another, just heaps of brick and mortar and twisted rusting machinery. Sometimes you see a piece of an upper floor, which somehow has never fallen down, with a bed still perched on it and the mattress still upon the bed, though walls and staircase and everything except the boards beneath have disappeared.

The communication trenches are very long and deep; it is difficult to find your way, in spite of the names, Waterloo Road, Strathcona Road, Sauchiehall Street, and so on, according to the fancy of the regiment which has made them. In places they are full of thistledown, which comes drifting in from the waste fields. My company was not in the actual fire-trench, so I had not much to do in the twenty-four hours while I was there. I had a fine bathe though, in deep clear water, which is a luxury you can't often get in the trenches.

My leave seemed very short when I got back; all those who have gone since got an extra day, so I was unlucky; but while the war lasts I would much rather be out here than at home, except for leave occasionally.

Billets : August 29, 1915.

I did not like leaving you alone in that crowd without your friends. I hope they came soon. Stainton I saw for about five minutes, and it was nice to see him looking so well again. I did enjoy that day in London with you, and I don't think we could have used our time better. M. is looking a bit older and thinner since the war began, so are we all, I daresay, but it strikes me again and again how very much easier it is for the men who come out here than for those who stay at home. The only real hardships and suffering —except of course actual wounds—come from the mind and not from the body, and the things which you imagine are much worse than what you actually see and hear.

It was strange to be back here at five o'clock on a misty August morning, with the sun just rising, and at lunch time I was in Chelsea again, in a Cheyne Walk which held a dressing station but not a hospital. It is an interesting part of the line ; there was a tremendous lot of fighting here just about Christmas and the New Year, and Tom cannot have been very far away when he was killed , now it is very much the same as any other place, except that there are more guns behind on both sides, and a greater maze of trenches. I am to be taken for a tour of inspection round the trenches to-morrow, and I'm looking forward to seeing them all. It's curious to see the heaps of waste from the coal mines dotted over the country ; the artillery observe from the top sometimes, but the mines are working not far back from the trenches, and I see the French miners going to and fro wearing round leather hats with wide brims, in which they put their lamps   I wish I could come across French guns and French troops.

Yesterday afternoon I had a bathe in a canal basin; some fine diving from a ruined engine-house about twenty feet above the water, but the bank was mainly coal dust, so that you came out much dirtier than you went in. It's curious how often the best soldiers are the men with a little enterprise, who are always keen to bathe, or to see some new place. If I had to choose my men like Gideon, and had never seen them before, I think I also would lead them down to the water's edge, and notice the men who undressed quickly and dived in; they would be the best.

This morning we had a long tramp round a perfect maze of trenches where even our guide seemed rather uncertain of his way, and it's not easy to recognise landmarks at the bottom of an eight foot trench; we saw a lot of curious things which I cannot tell you about : these battles in the trenches get more and more complicated every day, but in our last trenches I believe the Germans used to shout 'keep down Jock' before they opened fire with their machine-guns at night. They wanted to know if we were the Black Watch; they are very frightened of the Black Watch, since one memorable night last winter when the Black Watch chased a lot of them through a village and slew them with picks and spades. I walked into the local market town this afternoon; rather a fine square with old houses round about it, a belfry, and a fourteenth-century cathedral. It was a French town, distinctly not Flemish.

Well, I know now what you look at across the Forth, and I wish I could come along that sea-walk sometimes with you.

Billets · August 31, 1915.

We go back to trenches to-morrow, and I went down this afternoon to have a look at them. They used to be French trenches; the dug-outs are quite different from ours and much deeper under ground, and the different alley ways, instead of being called after London or Glasgow streets, are 'boyan' 14, 'boyan' 15, and so on. Our old friend the trench mortar was busy, but his bark is much worse than his bite, and we must try to shut him up. A Welsh regiment was in the trenches, and I saw this little poem written on a sand-bag:

> God makes bees,
> Bees make honey,
> The Welsh does the work,
> And the R.E. gets the money.

Of course engineers get higher pay than infantry,

though I don't quite know why they should in this war. There is a song, too, in this part of the line which all the troops sing as they come marching up the road to the trenches, but I only know the last three lines, which are—

The bullets and shrapnel they whistle and roar ;
I don't want to go to the trenches no more—
        I want to go home.

But they sing it cheerfully. We have four or five new subalterns since I was away on leave, but are still very short of senior officers.

Trenches : September 2, 1915.

So far we have had nothing very frightful in these trenches ; I am sitting in a dug-out about sixteen feet below the level of the ground, so that I feel safe against anything, except the very heaviest shell. We have a French miner's lamp with carbide in it to give us light, but for all that it's rather dark and stale smelling after so many months of habitation. The French have taken a lot of trouble to make these deep holes and prop them up, but they don't seem to have troubled themselves so much with the fire-trench. In places the Germans are only about thirty yards away, and they creep even nearer at night among the broken ground of the mine craters to throw bombs at us, and we do the same to them. I think either side might rush the other's front line at any minute, but they might find it hard work to stay there. The German trench mortars must have gone away, I think; at any rate we have seen none in the last twenty-four hours Both French and German ammunition is lying about, so I suppose the trenches changed hands more than once; they were very slippery last night after a few showers, and I hope we shan't be here through the winter, for these deep holes would simply become wells. There are a lot of blue corn-flowers growing in the long grass which hangs down into the trenches; a pretty blue vetch too.

Trenches . September 3, 1915

We had a new game this morning, ' hunt the General,' but I did not enjoy it very much, for I had only had three hours lying down, and had been up since 4. We were told the G O.C. 2nd Division would come round our trenches at 9.30, so for an hour I stood in a puddle waiting for him at the corner of my trench. I was cold and my feet were wet, and it was raining, and I'd had no breakfast, so I didn't bless him Then came rumours that he had been seen first in one trench and then in another; you wouldn't think a general and his staff could lose themselves like needles in a hay-stack, but for an hour I pursued him round and round our muddy rabbit warren, up one slippery trench and down another, while Campbell also tried to head him off. Finally, at 11.30, I gave up, and sat down to cold boiled eggs and tannin, the remains of breakfast. But he did come after all, along a back trench which never led him to this company. Then I slept my sleep until my bed-fellows made things uncomfortable. I caught ten to-day, a record bag; but I think I can get some powder for them when we go back to billets, as I hope we shall to-morrow. These trenches are not comfortable for a long stay, but they are very interesting.

Late last night I was sitting in the dug-out, reading by the dim lamp, when I heard a cheerful Scotch voice say, ' I've gotten a wee souvenir for ye.' I looked up, and there was a German standing in the doorway, in grey cap and tunic, with red piping. He was a deserter, a young Prussian who had crawled across in the dark into our wire, and when challenged put his hands up; then Fraser, our enormous subaltern, reached out a brawny arm, and swung him into the trench. He was not a bit frightened; he knocked some papers off a chair, sat down and asked for a cigarette. He was very anxious to talk, and I did wish my German had been better, so that I might have pumped him. He said he had come because it was 'better over here.' Two others crawled out with him; we captured one of them too, wounded by one of the German bombs as he lay in front, but I think the other must have gone back. He told me a good deal about the officers and sergeants and their strenuous life in billets, more in fact than I could understand, but we sent him in to headquarters and they would get all his information. He was a miserable creature—I do despise a deserter—no doubt he will be shot if he ever goes back to Germany; but it shows that even Prussians are losing heart if two of them desert in one night; he carried an ugly-looking knife, and had a photograph of his company in his pocket-book, with a football in front of them— six of them were wearing the iron cross.

It's a very wet night, and has been raining more or less all day, so that everything is ankle deep in mud and water, and we feel that the winter will soon be upon us; but evidently the Germans opposite dislike it much more than we do.

I read 'Cyrano de Bergerac' again the other day. What a fine play it is! I would have given anything to hear Coquelin declaim the great speech about his nose. Sometimes there seems to be so little in common between France to-day and the old France, until you realise how, in spite of all

U

changes of government, Frenchmen have clung to their great literary traditions, and have kept their fighting spirit. You know that first line of du Bellay's sonnet :

France, mère des arts, des armes, et des lois.

It was written about 1550, I suppose, and yet I think it must still express all that Frenchmen feel about France. An Englishman writing the same lines would put the three things in the reverse order of importance, don't you think ?

Billets : September 5, 1915.

About 8 last evening, a very draggled regiment of Highlanders, their knees the same colour as their khaki aprons, marched into barracks ; we were only three days in the trenches, but the mud was ankle-deep in places owing to the wet weather, and a heavy shower just before we were relieved made things worse. It took an hour's wading to get clear of the trenches at all, and then we had seven miles to march on a paved road. But the men knew they were going to good billets, and were pleased to get out of that warm corner. I heard one of them say, as the mud flowed round his legs, ' That's the way I like ma parritch, weel thickened.'

We had a bit of bad luck the night before,

and lost six men and an officer all wounded by the same bomb ; the wounded subaltern only came to us a month ago from the Glasgow Highlanders, a very nice fellow. It was a terrible job to get them out, down narrow twisting slippery trenches in the dark, for they were all wounded in a sap head, only ten yards from a German sap, and one of the wounded men made rather a fuss. The Germans could hear our stretcher-bearers ploutering about in the mud, and this man would not keep quiet, though he wasn't really badly hit, so, of course, as soon as anyone moved they threw more bombs in twos and threes ; however, after a couple of hours, we did get them all away, and I think they will all recover. We had only one man killed besides, in spite of constant rifle-grenades, bombs, and trench mortars ; but we had a trench mortar battery too, which made far more noise than the German one, and we heard the Germans yelling in terror when its first bomb went off.

B company have been unlucky since I joined them ; out of six officers killed and wounded since I came out, four have been ours, and since Bankier went to be adjutant, I am the only one left who was there in February.

It was strange after leaving the trenches at 5 o'clock to find myself at 8 in a comfortable bedroom with sheets and hot water, the best billet

U 2

I have had yet. My hostess is a *vieille fille* who had billeted some of us when I was home; she had heard about our two German prisoners, so we told her that Fraser, the large man, had caught them one in each hand by the collar. She was very much disappointed that we hadn't killed them. I don't wonder that French women hate the Germans like vermin.

To-day was fine and clear and sunny, with a suggestion of autumn. I walked over to see Glass in the clearing hospital. He's going on well, but has nine holes in him. The hospital was close to a landing place for aeroplanes; it was wonderful to see them coming down in steep spirals, shining in the sun; sometimes they seemed to dive almost straight downwards, and then to turn on their edge until they almost turned over.

The hospital was in a pretty château, next door to a sugar beet factory, but the trees and grounds were much older than beet-sugar, and I think there had been an old abbey there—perhaps it was destroyed in the Revolution. It was a very clear day, I could see the puffs of bursting shells on the top of a pit-heap miles away; the Germans must have been shelling an observing station.

Billets : September 7, 1915.

To-day I had a curious experience, for I walked a few miles across country to see if I could find that château which Tom described in his last letter. It was a beautiful September day, and I was able to take short cuts across the stubble fields, close beneath one captive balloon with its midget in the basket slung below. I found the village, but it was so full of troops that I did not expect to find the French owners still in their house ; however, when I came up the drive, there was a French lady sitting with her sewing on the verandah, so I told her why I had come and showed her the post-card. She remembered that night very well, because from then until the beginning of June she had billeted no British officers, though plenty of French ; she remembered Captain Wilson Smith's name, and Tom too, though not by name. I saw one of the daughters, quite a pretty girl. There had been nine of them there that night, and they marched away very early, for their orders were to rendezvous at Lille ; but she had told them that the Germans were close, and that they were forty-eight hours too late. She had met the sergeant-major of the K.O.S.B.'s some weeks later, and he told her they had almost all been killed.

Unfortunately, two French officers arrived in

their car before I had time to ask her name, but I thanked her before I left for having been so kind to Tom. The officers were friends whom they were expecting, so I did not like to stay. It was a very charming spot ; a double-storied house painted white, with green wooden shutters, and a broad verandah running the length of the house, and looking out upon the garden just the view in Tom's post-card ; there were ducks and water-fowl swimming in the pond, and some beds of flowers. I would have liked to stay there longer; perhaps another day I will show them his photograph which I had not with me.

I am billeted just beside a canal, which would be pleasant for an early morning bathe, if it was not so fearfully dirty ; I really can't face it. . . .

Read Mr. Balfour's letters whenever you see them in the papers; they are very good, and full of the most delightful irony, which is refreshing among so much bluster and indignation.

It rather amuses me to see how much value the Germans put on American threats. The Americans will soon begin to realise that everyone takes it for granted that they won't fight, and that they could not do very much for the first year if they did, and their pride will resent that, even though at present they don't seem to have quite enough.

Billets : September 8, 1915.

Another day of rest and sunshine. I told Daisy yesterday how I had found Tom's château and seen the lady who entertained him so hospitably. It seems hard that in those first weeks of war they should have had so little rest, as well as all the fighting ; now many officers have beds in the trenches, and most of them grumble if they do not get a bed and sheets in billets ; yet he had only the one night in bed, and had to march at two in the morning. If you have a copy of Tom's letter, I think that French lady would like to see it, if I get a chance to go over there again.

To-day I marched a party to the baths, where they got a change of raiment—no doubt just as necessary to the Patriarchs as it was to them—and all the kilts and jackets were fumigated ; I had a fine hot bath myself too. This afternoon I had a ride for a couple of hours, and wish I had done it before, for though I am no horseman, I can enjoy it. On the way I met a man who used to be in college at Winchester with me.

I am in command of B company at present, for Campbell went home on leave this morning ; he only came out again at the end of May, so he has not had long to wait.

Billets : September 10, 1915.

We still have brilliant September days, but there is a keen strong north wind to-day which makes the distances clear ; better weather for the artillery, which is very important here ; we have not been called upon for digging parties or other fatigues in this billet.   We are well away from the firing line, so that shells don't worry us, and we spend the mornings in training, and lead a peaceful sleepy life in the afternoon.   I rode over yesterday to the 56th Brigade Headquarters to see if I could find Billy Mitchison ; he's signal officer to that brigade, but unfortunately he was out. I hope he may come to see me some day.   We are what is called Inlying Picquet, which means that we have to be ready to move at a few minutes' notice, so I can't go over to see him myself.

I quite enjoy commanding the company.   In billets, as a rule, it only means paying out and sending a good many messages and signing papers ; but in action it is a big responsibility to have to watch 200 men as best you can, and I have only one subaltern at the present time.

We spent most of the morning scratching like hens in a stubble field with entrenching tools, trying new schemes for marking out trenches quickly; but it's one thing to do it by day-light and quite another thing to do it in the dark under fire.

Billets : September 12, 1915.

The brigade moves back into trenches to-morrow, but we, I fancy, are in support and not in the firing line. There should be no great hardship about that if this fine sunny weather lasts. Church parade to-day in a stubble field; we have a new padre, a nice fellow, but when he suggested to the men that the conservation of energy and the indestructibility of matter were arguments telling in favour of future life, I think he might as well have been preaching to the aeroplanes for all they understood.

This afternoon I walked up a hill, or rather a slight rise in the ground, and had a fine view of Bethune across the plain; its square cathedral tower and pointed belfry are landmarks for miles in this level country, but the hills and woods begin not far to the south. There was nothing in the view of corn-fields and orchards to suggest war at all, but I wish we could fight hard every day for a couple of months and get it over, instead of waiting eternally. Some of the men now think, as I see by their letters, that Kitchener is in command out here—' a big rough man with a wild eye on him,' as one of them described him after marching past him. Most of their letters are full of the same old phrase, ' hoping this finds you as it leaves me,' and ' drawing to a close ' when the stock is exhausted, but one or two always write excellent letters. ' Dear Wife, the pies you sent me last week had hair on them when I got them ' was a good way of explaining what had happened in the hot weather.

The French bean harvest is now in full swing; there are fields and fields of them, so they really do come from their name-place, unlike the Jerusalem artichoke ; they leave them until they are turning yellow, then pull up the plants by the roots, gather them in great bundles, put a stake through the middle, and leave them to dry in the fields. We used to see these bundles in between the trenches in several places, and if you didn't take particular notice of them by day, you were very apt to mistake them for Germans by night.

Billets : September 11, 1915.

We're still having beautiful weather, starry nights and sunny days and misty mornings, and the men have had a better rest than at any time since I came out. I was very glad to see Booth's Military Cross, and it must have been a very fine bit of work. I admire that sort of thing more than the one plucky effort which is all over for good or bad in a moment ; you want men who can act quickly, but you also want men who can stick to their job for hours under a heavy fire, especially in this war. But our fighting here since May can have been nothing compared with the Dardanelles, where you come under shell fire a mile or two out to sea, and once you land, you can never hope to escape from it at all, and there are no billets to go to, and no leave, and little enough food and shade and water. It must be a regular hell for everyone who is not in a ship.

Billets · September 13, 1915.

We have not gone into trenches after all, but only to new billets—some rather squalid cottages beside a grimy canal; they will do well enough if the weather keeps fine, but in winter they must stand in a swamp. The wind has gone round to the west, so I'm afraid our fine weather may break up. The 2nd H L I. were to come into our old billets, but they had not arrived when I left.

September 15.—I began this letter two days ago, and never finished it ; various odds and ends of work for the company have filled up the evenings. Yesterday I was nearly arrested as a spy, while I was making a reconnaissance of some swampy ground for the Colonel, to see if we could find a better path across it. It was so funny that I found it very hard to answer questions without laughing, but in the end I did convince a suspicious old colonel that I was what I pretended to be. He was quite right, for I don't think we are nearly careful enough about spies—a man with a little cheek could go anywhere and see anything. The swamp was rather a pretty place, with long reeds and marsh plants, and I disturbed a kingfisher from a tree trunk which had fallen across a ditch. This morning I went again, this time with Wardlaw Ramsay to protect me, and on the way I met Quiller-Couch, the novelist's son, who used to be at Winchester and Trinity, now he is Adjutant to an R.F.A. Brigade. We walked a long way, but I can't say we found any very good paths; the old tracks show up very white when the grass gets trodden down into mud and then dries, so that the German aeroplanes photograph them, and then the German guns make a point of shelling them; no doubt we do the same to them.

Billets : September 16, 1915.

How nice it is to hear of you with your sailors and soldiers ! I envy you your chance of getting to know so many of them in their natural selves.

It's very difficult for an officer to do that, for somehow his main occupation seems to be finding fault ;
there's so little to praise in the trenches, and so
much to do wrong, or do slackly ; also the tradition
of our army is, that officers are one kind of animal,
and men another, and you can't break that down.
Men have so little imagination too, that on quiet
days, or safe in billets, they will quite forget what
might happen at any moment if discipline or pre-
cautions were neglected. But in hospital it must
be quite different and pleasanter. . . .

I walked into the town to-day, and had a bath,
for we go back into trenches to-morrow. I have
had a lot of walking, for yesterday I went round
and round just out of rifle range behind the trenches,
trying to find out all the paths through a bit of
swamp ; it was very hot, and very difficult to plan
them all out, and now we are going to different
trenches after all, so that my labour is wasted.
It was difficult ground for troops, though it would
have been a nice little corner for snipe and ducks
in winter, just like these long stretches of marsh
which you see between Calais and Amiens on the
way to Paris.

I met young Quiller-Couch, who used to be at
Winchester with me, and I think stroked one of
Tom's trial eights, and twenty yards further on
there was another link with the literary world,

the grave of Marion Crawford, the novelist's son, a Lieutenant in the Irish Guards.

To-day I see from a paragraph that G. L. Cheeseman has been killed at the Dardanelles, a very great loss to New College, and to me, for he was very much more than my tutor. . . . He was a most loyal and honest friend, and gave everyone who knew him something of his own passion for learning, and hatred of repeating other people's ideas at second-hand. He loved enterprise—in travel, food, literature, politics, and everything else—but for him you would never have gone to Greece. He was a really fine historian, and, by the irony of fate, he had a great respect for Germans and German scholarship, and rather a contempt for the modern Greeks and Italians, whom he classed as ' Dagoes.' But, like many scholars, he had an intense admiration for men of action, especially for the Romans and the Roman Army, which was his great subject ; and I know he entered on this expedition to the Dardanelles with double zest, because he was fighting on historic ground, to win back the Roman Capital from the Turk. Now he lies like a scholar and a soldier beside the Hellespont ; but for me he will always haunt those rooms at New College where I have talked with him so often far into the night, of the places where he too fought, and the men who used to fight there. He wrote to me from his troopship on the way, reminding me of our reading-parties at Church Stretton—we used to gather there just at this time of year before the Oxford term began —and saying how different we should all be when we met there again. It's true, but I'm afraid the half of us will not be there at all. I feel that death has been kind to him, for he was given the very place and time which he himself would have chosen ; he would have hated growing old, and he had a horror of settling down, which made him often chafe against the routine of Oxford.

It's nearly 10, and we are inlying picquet to-night, and so I am saved all the trouble of undressing or taking off my boots.

♭

Trenches : September 17, 1915.

I am back at my old occupation, climbing round the trenches in the dark visiting the sentries ; we are in the same trenches again, but this time another company has taken over the favourite place for bombs. We relieve some of the K.R.R. I thought I knew one of their captains by sight, and he suddenly said to me, 'Do you remember Thule ? ' He had been one of my juniors in Thule Chamber, when I was in college.

So far it is dry, thank goodness, so the trenches are very different from what they were when we left them. Campbell is not back from leave yet; I hear that the Channel boats are temporarily stopped, so that mails may be irregular too; certainly none came to us yesterday, and your copy of Tom's letter arrived too late the day before for me to take to the French lady; perhaps I shall get another chance, as the place is not very far away.

We have some rifles with periscopes attached for firing over the top of the trench; the difficulty is, not in the sighting, but in overcoming the kick of the rifle, for, as you know, when the butt isn't held firmly into the shoulder, the rifle will jump when it is fired, and the shot will go high and wild, and it's difficult to prevent that without a vice to hold it. The number of devices for killing men employed by both sides at the front is extraordinary; we have about a dozen different kinds of bombs, besides trench-mortars, drain-pipe mortars, rifle grenades, and of course every kind of shell.

Trenches: September 19, 1915.

Night watches leave time for letter-writing, and the night is ever so much longer now, as we know to our cost. We have been digging a new bit of trench—it was behind our front line, but still not more than 150 yards from the Germans—and it always amuses me to notice how men dig when they find themselves in the open with bullets coming over; you should see the earth fly. I would do the same myself, if I had a spade, for after living under cover so long you feel almost naked in the open. In three hours' work, even in the dark, a man will do as much as takes a navvy a whole day at home. It was very hot to-day, but I found a place where I could look out far toward the German side without being seen, and the pitiless sunshine showed up the country in its desolation; the long grass is withered now, and the ears of corn bleached and draggled; there are still a few poppies and corn-flowers here and there, but otherwise the prevailing colour was a dirty yellow. In the distance were some rows of dead trees—either their bark had been ringed to make firewood in the winter, or else the bullet holes had bled them to death, as I have often seen happen—and they grouped themselves round the skeleton of a farm, roofless, windowless, just a mass of ruined brick-work. Our guns were shelling the German parapet, raising enormous clouds of dust and greenish smoke, and they were also battering at a ruined village about a mile away, with heavy howitzers; you would hear the report of the gun, and the quiet whistling of the shell overhead, and then suddenly some house would disappear in a cloud of brick dust and black smoke. Then as the cloud slowly drifted away

x

down wind, the crash would come to your ears, and you would see the house emerge again without a roof and one of its sides completely gone. There was not a sign of life in all that village, it was like breaking all the bones in a dry skeleton ; if only the Germans could suffer that in their own country, instead of inflicting it on France and Belgium and Russia.

Alastair Campbell came back this morning, bringing with him a melon, the smell of which, mixed with the even stronger smell of mouse, fills the dug-out as I write. We have only six feet of earth on the top of us here, and a little porthole window to give light, on a level with the bottom of the trench.

Billets : September 21, 1915.

We came out of trenches last night ; only a short spell this time, but a busy one, and I seemed to spend half my time showing lost men and officers their right way in the trenches, for everyone loses their way in that maze. It was beautiful weather, very clear, so that you could see every stick and sand-bag in the German lines for miles. We must have had at least eight miles to march last night, a long way when men are tired and short of sleep, but for some reason everyone was very cheerful and musical ; my platoon formed itself into a

regular whistling band ; as one of them remarked,
'There must ha' been canary seed in the parcels
last mail.' A great favourite is a song which only
has two lines that I can hear—'Wash me in the
water that you wash the dixies in and I shall be
whiter than the snow.' 'Dixies' are camp kettles.
I was also very much tickled with one remark.
We passed a pioneer battalion of Seaforths, who
had abandoned the kilt and were wearing khaki
shorts. I remarked that it would make some of
the veterans from the 72nd and 78th turn in their
graves, if they saw their old regiment in that dress.
'Ay, ye may say that,' said one man, 'for there's
some of they Seaforths is born in kilts ; ye mind auld
McRae o' this regiment, he was sae Hielan' ye
could see the heather grawin' oot o' his lugs.'

We are back near our old billets where we rested
ten days ago, a nice farm with a cool airy mess,
free from flies and very clean. I have a very
comfortable bed, and my only regret is, that to-night
I have to go digging, so I shall probably spend
very little time in it There is a stream of water
near—a rarity in Flanders—and a canal for the
men to bathe in, and an orchard full of trenches,
though it is miles behind the firing line. We still
have beautiful September weather, but for the last
two days the guns have been thundering away to the
south—all night too. The sound of them is like the

roll of kettle-drums—that must be the French 75's, I think. The Germans opposite must wish they had never been born.

Two more brace of grouse arrived the other day ; unfortunately they were just ' past.' The mail had been delayed a day, then the parcel had lain for twenty-four hours in a farm behind the trenches, and, finally, my bright servant never told me when it arrived, but left it for a night and a morning on the side of the trench, in the sun ; there are times when I feel that stupidity is the only vice, and that I don't care what else a man does, if he will use common sense. . . .

I believe the Zeppelins were a most beautiful sight, coming out from behind the clouds in the distance like a shoal of goldfish, and as they came nearer, sailing along like golden cigars with searchlights playing on them, and shells bursting all round. . . . Yesterday I saw nine aeroplanes in a flock—a battle squadron—I think, and it was intensely interesting to see them turn and manœuvre as they came under fire from the German anti-aircraft guns. They swung this way and that, but I think they all got through the danger zone, and sailed away behind the German lines—a raiding expedition, I expect. We shall get a ' hurl ' in motor lorries to our digging to-night, so we oughtn't to have very far to tramp.

Billets : September 23, 1915.

Last night three officers and 120 reluctant men were ordered to go out digging, so we marched for a couple of miles and then piled into a great string of motor lorries, which took us down to the trenches. It was a change for the men, and the road was crowded with Highlanders and other Scots, so that there was a running fire of chaff all the way, and insults in broad Scotch hurled back and forward. Most of this Kitchener Army Scottish Division have got khaki Tam-o'-shanters, and some of them are in khaki kilts. Lochiel's Camerons look very smart, and no doubt they have a great opinion of themselves. It was a beautiful still night with a full moon, but our artillery were keeping up a very heavy bombardment all through. We were set to work on a silly job some hundreds of yards behind the trenches, deepening a trench which seemed quite deep enough already, so that practically all we managed to do was to cut all the artillery wire between the batteries and the trenches. That soon brought furious gunners buzzing about us; but really the men couldn't help it when they were never told the wires ran along the bottom of the trench, but were set down to deepen it in the dark. It was most comforting to listen to our guns—sometimes there was almost one continuous roar of shells leaving the guns and bursting far away, with a swish like a waterfall as they rushed overhead. I climbed up to a place where I could see the bursts of flame far and near over the level country, and long afterwards the deep ' cr-rump ' of the shell came to my ears ; a lot of houses had been set on fire, and were blazing fiercely, so that it was a weird and wonderful sight ; and sometimes there would be a minute of complete silence— still moonlight and the mist rising from the hollows— and then with a flash and a roar the guns would open again. The Germans were hardly sending anything back ; no doubt they were biding their time. Finally, we gathered our tools and marched back to our lorries. It was very cold for an officer in a kilt on the front seat, though warm enough for the men who were packed like herrings behind. We had a bit of a march at the end too, so we didn't get to bed until 2.30 A.M.

I woke up with the sound of ducks quacking in the farm-yard just outside ; they seemed to have an intolerable lot to say, and as I lay I noticed the most gigantic Daddy-long-legs I have ever seen on the ceiling above me. It suddenly occurred to me, what on earth can he use his legs for ? They are far too long, and the joints all go the wrong way ; he has wings, so he needn't use them for wading ; perhaps they act like the tail of a kite to keep him

steady on the wing, but in that case it would have
been better to give him a better pair of wings. Or
perhaps, like Malvolio he thinks his long slim legs are
irresistible to Granny-long-legs. If Darwin's right,
there must be some purpose in his legs to fit him
to survive, but I can't see it; they are like the
appendix.

This is a very pleasant place for short strolls
on these fine moonlit evenings, along the edge of
the canal. Whole families live on board the barges,
and you see the smallest boys and girls steering.
One barge, very neat and clean, had the curious
name 'Mon Idée' and then the owner's name;
but I think he might have given credit to Noah,
for surely it was *his* idea first.

Trenches : September 24, 1915.

MY DEAR DADDY,—This is your birthday, I
think, but this trench has not provided me with a
present for you as Laventie did for Mother.

We had an eight-mile march down last night,
an extraordinary hot night, hotter than any I
remember this summer. There was a lot of R.E.
material—timber and so on—to carry up, and just
as we reached the end of our mile-long communication trench, down came the rain. Of course in
five minutes every one was wet through and up to

the eyes in mud, and it was terrible work to carry these heavy timbers up in slippery darkness, with only the flashes of lightning to help. The thunder drowned the sound of the guns, which is saying a lot, for they have never ceased night and day lately, and there is a tremendous bombardment of the German trenches going on as I write.

We got everything up in the end, though it was worse than moving furniture at Thuluchan, and we are beginning to dry now, though last night was rather uncomfortable; unfortunately, the men can light no fires in these trenches, it's too near the Germans, but they had a ration of rum this morning to cheer them up.

Before long I think we shall be in the thick of it, for if we do attack, my company will be one of those in front, and I am likely to lead it ; not because I have been specially chosen for that, but because someone must lead, and I have been with the company longest. I have no forebodings, for I feel that so many of my friends will charge by my side, and if a man's spirit may wander back at all, especially to the places where he is needed most, then Tom himself will be here to help me, and give me courage and resource and that cool head which will be needed most of all to make the attack a success. For I know it is just as bad to run into danger use-lessly as to hang back when we should be pushing on.

It will be a great fight, and even when I think of you, I would not wish to be out of this. You remember Wordsworth's ' Happy Warrior ' :

Who if he be called upon to face
 Some awful moment to which heaven has joined
Great issues, good or bad, for human kind,
Is happy as a lover, and is attired
With sudden brightness like a man inspired.

Well, I never could be all that a happy warrior should be, but it will please you to know that I am very happy, and whatever happens, you will remember that.

Well, anything one writes at a time like this seems futile, because the tongue of man can't say all that he feels—but I thought I would send this scribble with my love to you and Mother.

Always your loving

BEY.

' Then I entered into the Valley of the Shadow of Death, and had no light, for almost half the way through it. I thought I should have been killed there, over and over ; but at last day broke, and the sun rose, and I went through that which was behind with far more ease and quiet.'—From Bunyan's ' Pilgrim's Progress,' a book A. D. G. had with him at the front, and which came home in his kit with a mark at the page of which this was the closing sentence.

'Nineteen'

Up thro' the sand and heather
  I climbed the stony track,
Then, where the valley ended,
  I turned, and I looked back.
A spring of water chuckled
  Among the bracken fern,
Far off the last light glinted
  Upon the winding burn.
In the still breath of evening
  The air was strangely cool,
The small gnats danced a measure
  Above each dimpled pool.
The steep bare hills had gathered
  Shadows in every fold,
Between the clear-cut headlands
  The sea was shining gold.
A faint and fitful murmur
  Carried the slow swell's roar,
One wisp of smoke climbed upwards
  Above the distant shore.
Then, as I looked and lingered,
  The gold was turned to grey,
And out into the silence
  A boy's heart fled away.
Sadly I turned homeward
  To leave that lonely place,
The valley was behind me,
  And the night was in my face;

For coming years may bid me
  Be merry and be wise ;
But nothing can recover
  That glory for my eyes.
And down that westward valley
  Among the hills of joy
There wanders, blithe and singing,
  The glad heart of a boy.

A. D. G.

(In the Island of Hoy,
      September 1908.)

AT THE BALLANTYNE PRESS
PRINTED BY SPOTTISWOODE, BALLANTYNE AND CO. LTD.
COLCHESTER, LONDON AND ETON